THANK YOU to Susanne Woods for believing in me and being there every step of the way in making this beautiful book a reality. To Holly DeGroot for gorgeous styling and photography, and to Kari, Shea, Rae Ann and the entire Lucky Spool team.

A big thank you to my husband who always supported and encouraged my love (and need) to create, and to my mom, crafter extraordinaire, who taught me the value of handmade.

Thank you to my online community, I couldn't do what I do without you all. Your enthusiasm and support for my work mean the world to me.

W0008409

CONTENTS

To Ferris, Melissa, and Ryan

INTRODUCTION

I love sewing. Love, love, love!!! It's my most favorite thing to do and I'm beyond excited that I get to share a book of my very own projects with you all.

Unlike so many amazing makers I know, I wasn't creative as a child. I was actually pretty bad in art class and have always thought of myself as completely lacking any imagination or creativity. So, when I came across some gorgeous handmade bags on Etsy back in 2011, I totally surprised myself by deciding to jump in and give sewing a try.

Even though my first projects weren't anything amazing and I cringe a bit when thinking about all those wonky seams and skipped stitches, I absolutely loved being able to make something I could actually use. Before I knew it, I was completely hooked. Soon after that I started my blog www.sotakhandmade and I was blown away by the generosity and support I found in our online community.

I carried on sewing like there was no tomorrow and spent every spare minute rushing to my machine to get at least some stitches in before my kids needed me. In fact, I sewed so much every night after I put my children in bed, that my youngest son could no longer fall asleep if he didn't hear the hum of my machine. How is that for being obsessed?

It's been 7 years now since I made my first tote bag and I have since started designing and selling my own patterns, but you know what? I still enjoy sitting at my sewing machine and whipping up a pouch, a tote or maybe even a quilt here and there as much as I did when I first discovered this fabulous craft.

So, whether you're just a beginner sewist, a seasoned veteran or somewhere in between, I hope this book inspires you to sew something for yourself, your home or even your furry babies.

Happy sewing, friends!

MY
FAVORITE
THINGS

FAVORITE TOOLS

CUTTING MAT, ROTARY CUTTER, AND ACRYLIC RULER: These are a must for precise cutting of pattern pieces. Make sure to replace your rotary cutter blade often (I change mine every few weeks) as it will give you more accurate cuts while being gentler on your wrists.

FABRIC SCISSORS AND UTILITY SCISSORS: Good, sharp scissors are also a must. Make sure to never ever use your fabric scissors for cutting anything else but the fabric, as it will dull the blades. I always keep a pair of cheap scissors on hand near my sewing area for when I need to cut paper or even cut through zippers.

SEAM RIPPER: We all make mistakes and a sharp, easy-to-hold seam ripper is every sewist's best friend. Don't shy away from using your seam ripper when needed. It's better to fix your mistake right when it happens than to ignore it and end up with a finished project you might not be quite happy with.

FABRIC MARKING PEN: My absolute favorite is Mark-b-Gone pen. It has a blue (water soluble tip) and purple (air soluble tip). I use the blue tip when I need the marks to stay in place longer, and I get rid of them by spraying on a bit of water once I'm finished. The purple tip is perfect for making very temporary marks that will disappear quickly.

HERA MARKER: This is a tool that makes a temporary but long-lasting thin crease or indentation in fabrics. I love using it to mark quilting lines instead of using a pen.

PINS: My favorite pins are crystal glasshead ones as they are long, wonderfully sharp, slide through fabric beautifully and don't leave any marks when removed.

SEWING CLIPS: These babies easily hold thick/many layers of fabric together. Perfect for times when pins just won't do, as they could damage or distort the fabric. Plus, they are fabulous at holding a quilt binding in place while you stitch.

THIMBLE: I do quite a bit of hand stitching and a good thimble protects my fingers. I like to use leather thimbles, but there are so many different kinds on the market. Try a few of them out and see which one feels the most comfortable for you to use.

FREEZER PAPER: Easy to see through which makes it a perfect choice for tracing templates and pattern pieces. Draw on the dull side, cut your shape out, and the shiny side will temporarily adhere to your fabric with hot iron pressing so you don't have to worry about your template shifting during tracing. Peel the template off and save it for the next time, as they are reusable.

MY HAND SEWING KIT: Some of my projects include a bit of hand sewing. Supplies you will need to complete those part of our projects are: a sharp hand-sewing needle, coordinating thread in the appropriate weight for your project, a thimble (see above) and a sharp pair of snips, fine-tipped embroidery scissors or similar small pair to cut threads.

FAVORITE MATERIALS

DESIGNER QUILTING COTTON: This 100% cotton fabric is such a delight to work with. It has a gorgeous smooth feel, irons well, has very little shrinkage after being washed and comes in an incredible array of prints and colors.

ESSEX LINEN: This is another one of my favorites because it is so versital. This cotton/linen blend is a bit more sturdy and textured than a solid quilt-store quality quilting cotton, but it is still easy to work with. It a perfect material for bags and pouches.

DUCK CANVAS: 100% cotton duck canvas is strong and thick with a bit of texture. It comes in many colors and is affordable, too. I love using it for my bags' linings as it gives the finished project just the right amount of stability and eliminates the need for extra interfacing.

PELLON SF101: This medium weight fusible woven interfacing is perfect to use with quilting cotton as well as linen fabrics, as it adds a bit more body without changing or altering the feel of the fabric itself. I'm totally hooked on this interfacing and I buy it by the bolt from my craft store to ensure I always have it on hand when needed.

THREAD: My favorite thread is a 100% polyester Gutermann sewing machine thread. I love that it comes in many colors, is available at my local craft store and I have never had any problems with breakage. Definitely a win-win in my book.

LEATHER STRAPS: I might be a bit obsessed with adding leather straps to my bags (and even some pouches at times). I buy my straps pre-cut — my favorite width is ¾", and I absolutely love the professional finished look they add to my projects.

RIVETS: One of my more recent discoveries, these are perfect for attaching handles and straps with a professional finish. Rivets come in quite a a variety of sizes and a few finishes, so that you can match rivets to the bag hardware you might be using.

A NOTE ABOUT SEAM ALLOWANCES:

All of the seam allowances are ¼" throughout, unless otherwise noted.

FAVORITE TECHNIQUES

QUILT AS YOU GO (QAYG)

The QAYG technique is my favorite way to use up randomly sized scraps. I recommend a 'controlled chaos' approach when working on QAYG projects, which means deciding in advance which color families to use and which to stay away from. If you organize your scraps by color, the scrappy fabric selection this technique employs will be even easier for you. Alternately, select a random assortment of any and every color you fancy for a super scrappy look

Once you have selected the scraps you want to work with, press them well before starting your patchwork. **(A)**

Next, select a batting. I like to use Warm and Natural because it is nice and thin. The QAYG projects in this book use the patchwork as a structured surface. Usually you want to create texture and some depth, but without adding a lot of bulk to the project itself. Because of this, I recommend avoiding polyester battings altogether due to the fact that they tend to have a higher loft (thickness).

Determine the size of the QAYG patchwork needed for the project you have in mind. I recommend starting with a bigger piece of batting than called for and trim the assembled panel as needed. The batting will need to be at least 1" or 2" larger on each side than your finished size. All of that quilting has a tendency to slightly distort the shape of the assembled panel.

Use the finished slab of patchwork as you would any piece of thicker fabric like a canvas or home dec weight fabric. These patchwork slabs usually won't need additional stabilizer either.

> **TIP:** Don't just use QAYG for the projects that I have used this technique for in this book. Use your QAYG patchwork slabs as the exterior for baskets, pouches, bags, potholders or even quilt blocks.

INSTRUCTIONS

1 Position one fabric scrap right side up in the center of the batting (just eyeball it, no precise measuring is needed). Smooth the scrap against the batting so that there are no puckers. Quilt using straight lines or as desired. Trim all the thread tails before moving on. **(B)**

> **TIP:** Use a walking foot if you have one. A regular presser foot will work fine, but you will need to sew slowly and smooth the fabric down as you sew to prevent puckering. I also recommend securing the fabric in place using a few pins if you are using a regular presser foot.

2 Position a second scrap right side down aligning it along one raw edge of the quilted scrap from Step 1. Attach using ¼" seam allowance. **(C)**

3 Position the fabric right side facing up and press the seam flat against the batting with your fingers. Add additional quilting on the right side of the fabric. **(D)**

4 Continue adding scraps all the way around your patchwork using this same technique until you have a big enough slab for your project. **(E, F)**

5 Press the entire quilted unit well before trimming to the desired size or cutting from it using a template as in the case of the QAYG Zipper Pouch (see page 22).

TIP: If a must-use scrap is not large enough to cover the desired area, simply add another scrap to it before attaching **(G)**. As the patchwork sides get longer, I stitch two or three different scraps into one longer piece and attach it as one unit. This gives the finished slab an even scrappier look and it uses up even my smallest cuts of fabric.

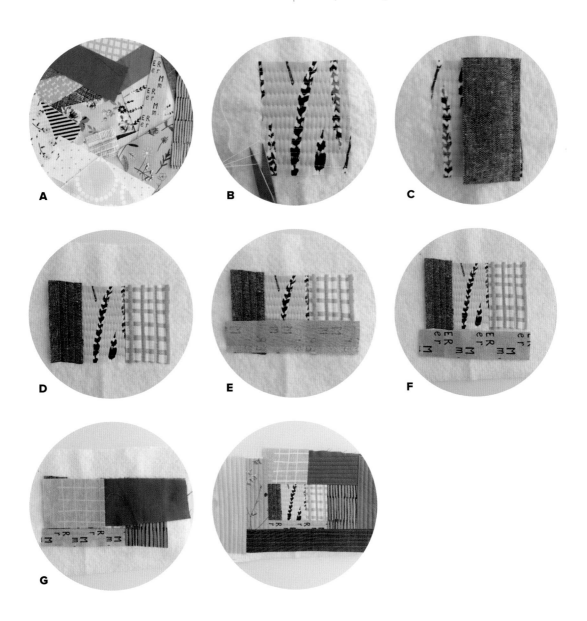

A

B

C

D

E

F

G

MAKING FABRIC HANDLES

I prefer using quilting cotton or Essex linen along with medium weight fusible interfacing to make my handles. Linen, twill or canvas will also work, but don't attach the interfacing if using one of these thicker fabrics.

First, determine the width of the finished handles and multiply this number by 4 to calculate the cut width of your handle strips. For example, if the finished handle is ¾" wide, cut the fabric strip 3" wide (0.75 x 4= 3).

For a 1" wide finished handle cut your fabric 4" wide (1 x 4= 4). Similarly, for a 1¼" finished handle, cut your fabric 5" wide (1.25 x 4= 5)...and so on.

If you have one, I recommend using a walking foot for topstitching and edgestitching handles, as it will ensure that all the fabric layers feed through evenly. Lengthen the stitch slightly and use a heavier weight thread, like 30wt, to make the stitching stand out, producing a more interesting finished handle.

INSTRUCTIONS

1 To make (2) ¾" wide x 14" long handles, cut (2) 3" x 14" strips of quilting cotton and (2) 3" x 14" strips of fusible interfacing.

2 Follow the manufacturer's directions to attach the fusible interfacing to the wrong side of both 3" x 14" fabric strips.

3 Fold one strip in half lengthwise, with the wrong sides together. Press. Open the strip again. Use the middle crease as a guide and, with the wrong sides facing, press the long, raw edges aligning each with the center crease. **(A)**

4 Fold the strip in half lengthwise again, enclosing the raw edges. Press and use clips to prevent layers from shifting. **(B)**

5 At the machine, hold both the top and bobbin threads with your fingers as you begin stitching. This prevents any knots from forming on the underside.

6 Edgestitch along the clipped, long edge first. Repeat along the folded long edge. I like to add an additional set of parallel stitches ¼" away from the edgestitching for added interest. **(C)**

7 Repeat to make a second handle.

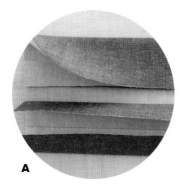

A

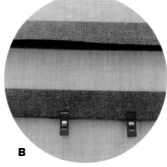

B

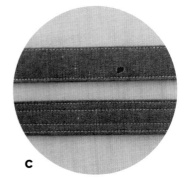

C

INSTALLING RIVETS

I'm totally smitten with using rivets to attach handles and straps to my finished bags and purses. I adore the professional look they add to handmade projects, especially when used with leather! These materials may not be in your sewing supplies already, but they are readily available at larger craft retailers or online. Maybe your local quilt shop has a set you can try out to see if you like them too before investing in your own. New hardware can be intimidating, so practice on a scrap of fabric first if you're new to working with rivets.

MATERIALS
rivets — my favorite ones are Dritz double cap 6-8mm rivets

leather hole punch

rivet setting tool — base and post

rubber headed mallet

water soluble pen

INSTRUCTIONS

1 Using the water soluble pen, mark the rivet placement positions on the strap. Use the leather hole punch to make neat holes in the marked positions. **(A)**

2 Working with one strap at a time, position the strap in the location desired on the finished bag. Using the water soluble pen and the holes in the strap as guides, mark each hole placement on the bag exterior. Move the strap aside and use the leather hole punch to cut neat holes in the fabric at the marks.

3 Align the leather strap over the holes in the bag exterior. Push the rivet post through both layers from the back. **(B)**

4 Place the base part of rivet setting tool, curved side up, on a flat wooden surface. Gently place the rivet cap on top making sure everything is neatly lined up.

5 With the metal post of the setting tool curved side down over the top of the rivet cap, use the mallet to hammer the top of the setting tool. Don't overdo it—three or four hits should be sufficient. Test to make sure the rivet is securely attached. **(C)**

6 Repeat Steps 1–5 for the rest of the rivets to secure your strap(s) in place.

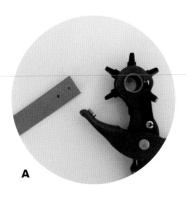

A

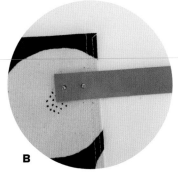

B

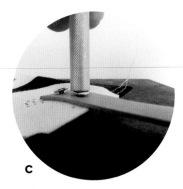

C

FOR
YOU

FOLDOVER POUCH

This adorable foldover pouch is quick for experienced sewists to make and a perfect project for someone giving pouch-making a try for the first time. With a small amount of fabric, a pretty button and an hour or two of your time, you can complete this sweet pouch.

FINISHED SIZE: 8½" wide x 6" tall when closed

MATERIALS

1 fat quarter of quilting cotton or Essex linen for the exterior

1 fat eighth of quilting cotton for the contrasting foldover flap

1 fat quarter of duck cotton canvas for the lining

Note: I used medium weight duck cotton canvas for the lining. Alternatively, use quilting cotton layered on the wrong side with a medium-weight fusible interfacing.

½ yard of medium weight fusible interfacing

(1) 4" length of ⅛" wide leather lace or ribbon

(1) 1" decorative button

perle cotton or strong, thick thread — 30 wt is great

hand sewing kit (see page 9)

fabric marking pen

acrylic ruler

fabric scissors

CUTTING

Note: the measurements below are width x height

From the exterior fabric, cut:
(2) 9" x 7" rectangles

From the flap fabric, cut:
(2) 9" x 4½" rectangles

From the lining fabric, cut:
(2) 9" x 11" rectangles

From the interfacing, cut:
(2) 9" x 7" rectangles
(2) 9" x 4½" rectangles

ASSEMBLING THE EXTERIOR PANELS

1 Following the manufacturer's instructions, fuse the interfacing to the wrong sides of both exterior panels as well as both flap rectangles.

2 Position an exterior panel and flap right sides together, aligning the 9" top edge of the flap with the top edge of the exterior. This way, the fabric won't be upside down when the pouch is closed if using a directional fabric. Pin and stitch along the raw edge. Press the seam towards the main panel, double topstitching along the pressed seam using a ⅛" and a scant ¼" seam allowance.

3 With the assembled unit from Step 2 right side up on the cutting mat, use a fabric pen to mark a 1" square along the two corners of the exterior and cut along the drawn lines. **(A)**

4 Repeat Steps 2-3.

5 Align both assembled exterior panels right sides together and pin or clip along both side edges and the bottom. Ensure that the seams between each assembled exterior and flap are aligned. Stitch along the pinned edges, backstitching at the beginning and end, leaving the corner cutouts from Step 3 unsewn. Press the seams open. **(B)**

6 Box the corners by reaching inside the exterior, pinching the unit and aligning the side and bottom seams. Stitch along the opening. Repeat on the other corner. **(C)**

7 Fold the length of leather lace in half to form a loop. Center the loop along the right side of the exterior back panel's top edge. Align the raw edges and baste in place using a ⅛" seam allowance. **(D)**

ASSEMBLING THE LINING

1 Mark and cut away 1" squares along both bottom corners of each lining panel in the same way as shown in Step 3 of Assembling the Exterior Panels.

2 Position the lining panels right sides together. Stitch along the two side edges and the bottom seam, leaving the corner cutouts frpom Step 1 unsewn. Leave a 3" opening in the bottom seam for turning the bag later. Press the seams open.

3 Box the corners of the lining the same way as shown in Step 6 above.

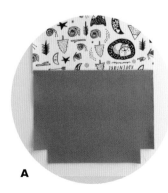

A

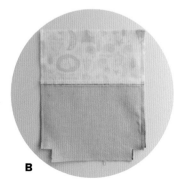

B

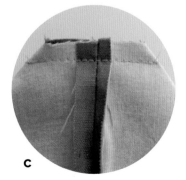

C

FINISHING

1 Insert the assembled exterior into the lining so that the right sides are facing **(E)**. Align the top raw edges as well as the side seams of the exterior and the lining. Make sure the button closure loop is tucked inside. Clip or pin all the way around the top of the pouch, keeping all the raw edges aligned.

2 Stitch around the top clipped edge of the pouch. Turn the pouch right side out through the opening in the lining. Stitch the gap in the lining closed by hand or machine and gently push the lining inside the assembled exterior.

3 Smooth the pouch's top edge with your fingers (roll the seam between your fingers to make it lay neat and flat). Clip the seam in place and topstitch making sure the loop is outside the pouch. **(F)**

ATTACHING THE BUTTON

Fold the pouch at the flap and bring over the button closure loop along the exterior. Mark the button placement using a fabric marking pen (the button will be centered about 1½"–2" away from the bottom edge of the pouch). Use the perle cotton and hand sewing kit to sew the button in place by hand.

CUSTOMIZATION TIP

Don't like the idea of an open top? Then consider adding a zipper to the top instead. To do this, cut (2) 4" x 1¼" rectangles from the flap fabric and gather an 8" zipper. Follow the instructions through Step 4 of Assembling the Exterior Panels and complete Step 1 of Assembling the Lining. Then, follow the instructions on page 24 of the next project to create the zipper tabs. Trim the excess tab fabric to align with the 9" edge of the exterior. Come back here to box all the corners and follow the Assembling the Zipper Pouch instructions on page 38 to complete the pouch.

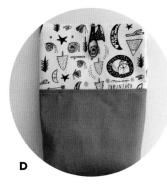

D

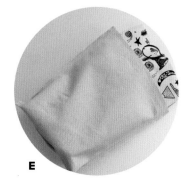

E

F

QAYG ZIPPER POUCH

Are you someone who likes to save even the smallest of your fabric scraps? Then this pouch is a perfect project for you. The main panels are constructed using the QAYG technique (see page 12) which makes for a beautifully structured pouch that is the ideal size to keep your pens, pencils, or even your make up organized in style.

FINISHED SIZE: 8" wide x 3" tall x 2½" deep

MATERIALS

(2) 13" x 7" rectangles of low loft cotton batting

enough QAYG scraps to cover both pieces of batting plus a bit extra

(1) 13" x 14" rectangle of quilting cotton for lining

(1) 13" x 14" rectangle of medium weight fusible interfacing

(2) 4" x 1¼" rectangles of quilting cotton for zipper tabs

(2) 2½" x 2" rectangles of quilting cotton for binding

(2) 2" lengths of ½" wide ribbon

(1) 11" metal or nylon zipper

leather for zipper pull (optional)

fabric marking pen

fabric scissors

sewing clips and/or pins

sewing machine zipper foot

ASSEMBLING THE EXTERIOR PANELS

1 Referring to the instructions on page 12, make two QAYG pieced units, each measuring 13" wide x 7" tall.

2 Using the Pouch pattern on page 122, cut two exterior panels out of the QAYG slabs. Baste all the way around the perimeter of both panels using a ⅛" seam allowance to secure the quilting. **(A)**

ASSEMBLING THE LINING PANELS

1 Following the manufacturer's instructions, fuse the interfacing to the wrong side of the 13" x 14" lining rectangle.

2 Using the Pouch pattern, cut two lining panels from the interfaced rectangle.

MAKING THE ZIPPER TABS

Note: I used two different fabrics for my tabs because I love the scrappy look. Feel free to use the same fabric for both tabs if you prefer.

1 Fold the short ends of the 4" x 1¼" zipper tab rectangle by ½" with the wrong sides facing. Press with a hot iron. Fold the pressed tab in half, wrong sides together and aligning the folded edges of the tab. Press again. Repeat for the second tab. **(B)**

2 With the two raw edges of one end of the zipper tape almost touching, stitch and backstitch over the tape ends a few times, about ¼" away from the zipper teeth. This will secure the end of the zipper tape closed and prevent it from shifting during assembly. Open up a pressed zipper tab rectangle and position the zipper tape inside the tab. Make sure the folded short edge of the tab comes as close as possible to the zipper stop. Refold the tab along the length, encasing the tape ends and aligning the short folded edges. Stitch in place using a ⅛" seam allowance. Trim the tab to the same width as the zipper tape. **(C)**

3 Repeat for the other end of the zipper tape.

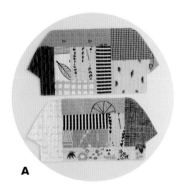

A

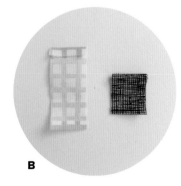

B

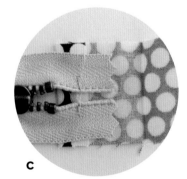

C

INSTALLING THE ZIPPER

1 On a flat work surface, place one exterior panel right side up. Center the assembled zipper right side down along the curved edge. Aligning the raw edges and working from the center out, pin or clip the assembled zipper in place and baste using ⅛" seam allowance. **(D)**

> **TIP:** You can clip into the zipper tape around the curved edges to help the zipper lay neater. Just make sure to clip into the seam allowance only. Don't cut the stitches!

2 Position the assembled exterior panel and the lining panel right sides together. Align the curved raw edges and pin or clip in place. Attach the zipper foot and stitch along the edge. Sew slowly when stitching around the curve to ensure that the line of stitching is as consistent as possible. Clip into the seam allowance around the curved edges making sure not to cut into the stitches. **(E)**

3 With the wrong sides facing, neatly press the exterior and lining panels away from the zipper. Topstitch through both the lining and exterior along the curved seam using a ⅛" seam allowance. **(F)**

4 Repeat Steps 1-3 to attach the second exterior and lining panels to the opposite long side of the zipper tape. Trim the excess fabric from the zipper tabs so they are flush with the sides of the pouch.

MAIN ASSEMBLY

1 Fold one length of ribbon in half and center it along one zipper tab aligning the raw edges. Baste the ribbon in place using a ⅛" seam allowance. Repeat with the second length of ribbon and the opposite zipper tab.

2 Open the zipper ¾ of the way. With the exterior panels right sides together, pin or clip the bottom raw edges neatly together. Attach a regular presser foot to your sewing machine and stitch along the bottom straight edge only, backstitching at the beginning and end.

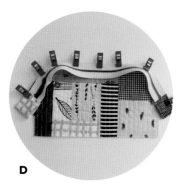

D

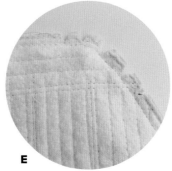

E

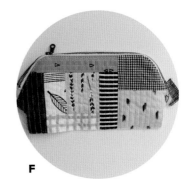

F

3 Repeat with the lining panels right sides together, only this time make sure to leave a 4" opening for turning. **(G)**

4 Turn the pouch wrong side out through the opening in the lining. Neatly align the exterior and lining side edges over each other with the ribbons nested between the panels. Clip or pin the side edges together and use a ⅛" seam allowance to baste along the sides of the pouch through all of the layers. **(H)**

5 Stitch the gap in the lining from Step 3 closed either by hand or by machine.

ATTACHING THE BINDING

1 With the wrong sides together, fold and press both long sides of the 2½" x 2" binding rectangles in by ¼". With the pouch still lining side out the zipper side facing down, align the raw edges of one folded binding rectangle with the pouch lining. You'll have the raw edges of about ½" of binding fabric extending on both sides. Attach the binding in place through all the layers and backstitching at the beginning and end.

2 Flip the pouch over. Fold the excess binding around the pouch's side edge. Holding the side folds in place, bring the long folded edge of the binding over to cover all of the raw edges of the pouch and the binding. Use clips to hold everything in place **(I)**. Topstitch along the fold on the binding through all of the layers, backstitching at the beginning and end to secure the stitching.

3 Repeat Steps 1-2 to attach the second binding to the remaining raw edge. Turn the pouch right side out and push the corners out to make them neat and pointy. Attach a thin strip of leather in the zipper pull if desired.

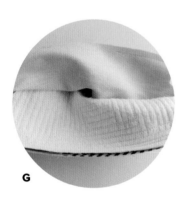

G

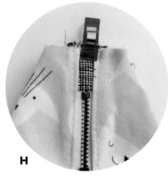

H

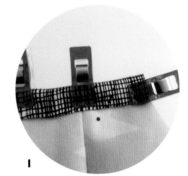

I

CUSTOMIZATION TIP

Once you have the hang of pouch-making, feel free to break out of the rectangle and create any shape you like. I used the same technique (minus the need for the binding) to create my Scissors Cosy and my Nina Wristlet.

Scissors Cosy

Nina Wristlet

PLEATED POUCH

Now that you have mastered a basic zipper pouch in a pretty shape, let's tackle pleats. This unique pouch features pleated sides that open up for extra room. Pleats might seem a bit intimidating at first, but you'll be surprised by how quickly this project comes together once you start sewing. In fact, choosing the perfect fabric and zipper combo might just be the most time-consuming task. :)

SIZE: 4½" x 8"

MATERIALS

fat quarter for main exterior

⅛ yard contrasting fabric

fat quarter for lining

⅓ yard medium weight fusible interfacing

(1) 14" nylon zipper

(1) 6½" length of ¼" wide leather strip or ribbon

utility scissors

sewing clips and/or pins

leather for zipper pull (optional)

CUTTING

Note: the measurements below are width x height

From the main exterior fabric, cut:
 (1) 11" x 9" rectangle for main exterior panel

From the contrasting fabric, cut:
(2) 1" x 9" rectangles for exterior strips
(2) 2½" x 5½" for binding

From the lining fabric, cut:
(1) 11" x 9" rectangle

From the interfacing, cut:
(1) 11" x 9" rectangle
(2) 1" x 9" rectangles

ASSEMBLING THE EXTERIOR PANEL

1 Following the manufacturer's instructions, fuse the interfacing to the wrong side of the main exterior panel as well as to both contrasting exterior strips.

2 Attach an exterior strip to both 9" edges of the main exterior panel, right sides together. Press the seam towards the strips and topstitch along the folded edge. Your main panel should now measure 12" x 9". **(A)**

INSTALLING THE ZIPPER

1 With the exterior panel and zipper tape right sides together, center the zipper teeth side down along one of the contrasting strip edges (if using a directional fabric make sure the top edge of the main exterior panel and the zipper pull are on the left edge). Align the zipper tape with the long raw edges of the contrasting strip. With the wrong side facing up, layer a lining panel on top so the zipper is sandwiched between the exterior panel and the lining. Align the raw edges and pin to hold in place. **(B)**

2 Stitch along the pinned edge using a scant ¼" seam allowance.

3 Press both panels away from the zipper and topstitch along the folded edge through all the layers using a ⅛" seam allowance. **(C)**

4 Bring the remaining 9" raw edge of the exterior panel up to align with the raw edge of the right side of the zipper. Pin or clip in place. Repeat with the lining and the wrong side of the zipper. **(D)**

5 Stitch along the pinned edge using a scant ¼" seam allowance.

6 Open the zipper all the way and press both panels away from the zipper, turning the project right side out so that the exterior and lining are wrong sides together. Topstitch along the edge of the zipper through all the layers using a ⅛" seam allowance (this step might be a bit tricky so stitch slowly to ensure the stitches are as neat as possible). **(E)**

7 Close your zipper about ¾ of the way and stitch a few back and forth stitches across both ends of the zipper using a ⅛" seam allowance. This prevents any shifting of the tape when assembling. Trim away any excess zipper tape using utility scissors. **(F)**

8 Position the leather or ribbon handle right side down along the pouch's top edge, ¼" away from the outside edge of the contrasting strip seam. Pin or clip to hold the handle in place and use a ⅛" seam allowance to stitch a few back and forth stitches to secure the handle. **(G)**

MAIN ASSEMBLY

1 Open the zipper about ¾ of the way and turn the pouch lining side out. Ensure the exterior panels are nice and smooth on the inside and fold the pouch in half centering your zipper. **(H)**

2 Clip the raw edges at both ends of the zipper to prevent the layers from shifting.

3 Fold both long side seams over by ¾", towards the zipper. Use clips or pins to secure the folds. **(I)**

4 Baste along both short raw edges using a ⅛" seam allowance backstitching at the beginning and end, and securing the folds as you sew. **(J)**

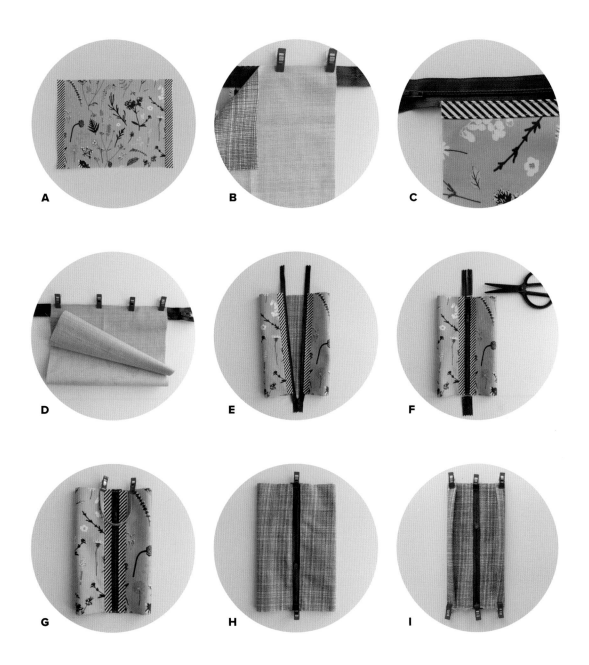

A

B

C

D

E

F

G

H

I

ATTACHING THE BINDING

1 With the wrong sides facing, fold and press both binding strips in half along their length. Position the assembled pouch, zipper side up, on the folded binding strip, aligning the raw edges. There will be about ½" of extra binding extending out on both sides. Attach the binding in place, backstitching at the beginning and end. **(K)**

2 Flip the pouch over.

3 Fold the excess binding around the pouch's side edge. **(L)**

4 Holding the fold in place, bring the long folded edge of the binding over to cover the raw edge of the pouch. Use clips to hold everything in place. **(M)** Repeat for the opposite edge.

5 Use a ⅛" seam allowance to stitch the binding in place, backstitching at the beginning and end. Repeat for the second raw edge with the remaining binding strip. **(N)**

6 Turn the pouch right side out, push the corners out to make them neat and pointy. Attach a zipper pull if desired. **(O)**

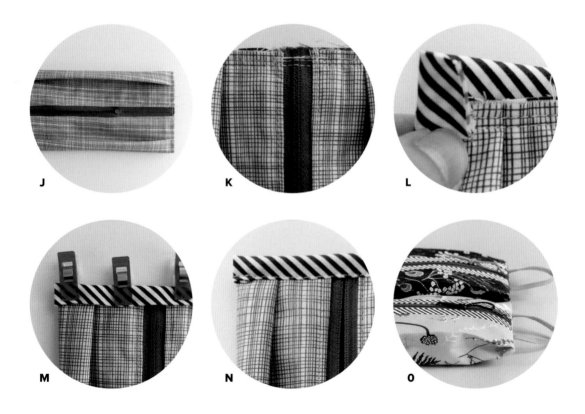

J

K

L

M

N

O

CUSTOMIZATION TIP

Consider adding a handy wristlet strap instead of a leather handle. To make a wrist strap and D-ring tab you will need:

(1) 2" x 17" strip of quilting cotton fabric

(1) ½" D-ring

(1) ½" swivel hook

1 Place a 2" x 17" strip of fabric right side down. Fold in half lengthwise, wrong sides together, press. Open the strip, press the long raw edges towards the middle.

2 Fold in half again and press (raw edges are hidden inside). Cut your strip into one 2" long strip and one 15" long strip. **(P)**

3 Pin the open edge of the 2" strip and stitch along both long edges using a ⅛" seam allowance. Pull the D-ring through the strip, fold in half, and stitch along the raw edge to form a loop. Set aside.

4 Pull the swivel hook through the 15" long strip making sure not to twist the fabric. Open both short raw edges, align them and pin together (right sides are together). Stitch along the pinned edge using a ¼" seam allowance and press the seam open. Your wrist strap forms one continuous loop now. **(Q)**

5 Refold the long raw edges towards the middle seam again, press. Use pins or clips to hold the layers together. Stitch along both folded edges using a ⅛" seam allowance.

6 Position the seam over the swivel hook and fold the strap in half. Use pins or clips to hold the strap edges aligned and stitch across the strap (going back and forth a few times) about ½" from the swivel hook to keep it from shifting. **(R)**

7 Attach the D-ring with its loop to the right side of the exterior panel of the pouch before sewing the exterior panels together. I usually attach it about 1" from the top edge. Add the wrist strap once the pouch is finished.

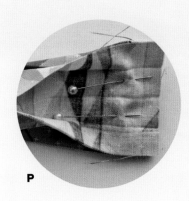

P

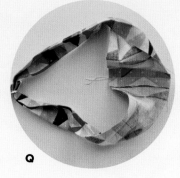

Q

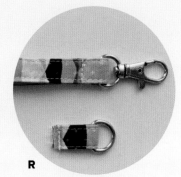

R

A PLACE FOR EVERYTHING CLUTCH

Sometimes all you need are a few essentials and you're ready to go. I designed this clutch for just this purpose. Inside you'll find plenty of room for your cards, cash and even your phone.

This fabulous clutch is one of the more time-consuming projects in this book though. I hope that won't discourage you from giving it a go. Just remember to read all the instructions before you start, measure twice and take things slowly. I'm sure you will love your finished clutch as much as I do mine.

FINISHED SIZE: 5" tall x 8¼" wide x 1" deep when folded

MATERIALS

Note: 1 fat quarter measures 18" x 21"

1 fat quarter of floral quilting cotton

1 fat quarter of black quilting cotton

1 fat quarter of blue quilting cotton

1½ yards of medium weight fusible interfacing

(1) 8" long zipper

(1) 7" long zipper

(2) heavy-duty snaps

sewing machine zipper foot

sewing clips and/or pins

fabric marking pen or fine chalk pen

small sharp fabric scissors

point turner

snap setting tool

leather for zipper pull (optional)

CUTTING

Note: *I recommend labeling all of the panels as you cut to prevent confusion. All the measurements are width x height.*

From the floral fabric, cut:
1 exterior Flap from the pattern on page 123
(1) 9" square for the slip zipper pocket panel
(1) 9" x 15" rectangle for the card slots

From the black fabric, cut:
1 lining Flap from the pattern on page 123
(1) 9" x 10" main exterior panel
(1) 9" x 6" rectangle for the main lining panel
(2) 8¼" x 3½" rectangles for the tall main panels for the zipper pocket

From the blue fabric, cut:
(1) 9" x 6" rectangle for the slip pocket lining
(2) 8¼" x 4" rectangles for the zipper pocket lining

From the interfacing, cut:
4 Flap panels from the pattern on page 123
(1) 9" square for the slip zipper pocket
(1) 9" x 15" rectangle for the card slots panel
(2) 9" x 10" rectangles for the main exterior
(1) 9" x 6" rectangle for the lower main lining
(2) 8¼" x 3½" rectangles for main panels for the zipper pocket

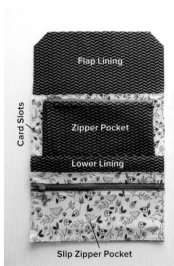

Flap Lining

Card Slots

Zipper Pocket

Lower Lining

Slip Zipper Pocket

Exterior Flap

Main Exterior

PREPARATION

1 Following the manufacturer's instructions, fuse the interfacing to the wrong sides of the floral slip zipper pocket panel, the card slots panel, the main lower lining panel and both of the main zipper pocket panels.

2 Fuse two layers of interfacing to both the exterior and the lining flaps as well as to the black main exterior panel.

ASSEMBLING THE ZIPPER SLIP POCKET

1 Subcut the slip zipper pocket panel into (1) 9" wide x 3½" tall rectangle and (1) 9" wide x 5½" tall rectangle.

2 With the 3½" tall rectangle from Step 1 right side up, center the 8" zipper along the top raw edge with the teeth facing down and the zipper pull on the left. Layer the 9" x 6" zipper pocket lining right side down on top, so the zipper is sandwiched in the middle. Align the raw edges and pin through all of the layers to prevent shifting. With the zipper foot attached to your sewing machine, stitch along the pinned edge, using a scant ¼" seam allowance. **(A)**

3 With the lining and main bottom panels wrong sides together, press away from the zipper. Switch to a regular sewing foot and on the right side of the slip pocket panel, edgestitch along the fold. Note that the pocket lining will be longer than the slip pocket panel. **(B)**

4 With the pocket lining right side up, bring the 9" raw edge up and align it with the top of the unsewn raw edge of the zipper tape and pin in place. Using a ⅛" seam allowance, baste along the pinned edge and along the side raw edges, to hold the pocket lining in place. Trim away any excess zipper tape to be flush with the side edges. **(C)**

5 Re-attach the zipper foot to your sewing machine. With the right sides facing, position the 5½" tall top pocket panel along the 9" edge of the assembled pocket, aligning the raw edges. Pin in place and stitch along the pinned edge, using a scant ¼" seam allowance. Note: If using a directional fabric, place the bottom edge of the pocket fabric along the zipper. **(D)**

6 Re-attach the regular foot on your sewing machine. With the top panel right side up, press away from the zipper and topstitch along the fold on the top panel, using a ⅛" seam allowance. **(E)**

7 Fold the pocket in half, wrong sides together, aligning the unsewn 9" raw edges. Using a hot iron, press the top fold (there should be about ¾" of exterior fabric visible above the zipper). **(F)**

8 Edgestitch along the fold of the pocket. With the right sides facing up, position the assembled pocket onto the black lower main lining aligning the bottom edges and clip or pin in place. Baste together along the bottom and side and set aside for now. **(G)**

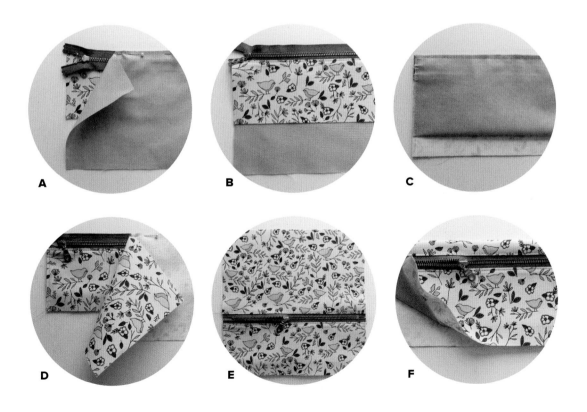

A

B

C

D

E

F

ASSEMBLING THE CARD SLOTS

1 With the 15" tall x 9" wide card slot rectangle right side up on a flat surface, use a ruler and a fabric marking pen to draw the following lines **(H)**:

Line 1: 3" from the top 9" edge

Line 2: 1¾" away from line 1

Line 3: 2¼" from line 2

Line 4: 1¾" from line 3

Line 5: 2¼" from line 4

Line 6: 1¾" from line 5

2¼" will be remaining on the bottom of the panel.

2 Begin ironing folds along the drawn lines, concertina-style. With the right sides together (first fold by hand and then press with a hot iron to set in place) fold along line 1. Next, fold and press along line 2, this time with the fabric wrong sides together, then the right sides together again, etc... Fold and press along all the rest of the lines to form three horizontal card pockets. **(I)**

3 Using a ⅛" seam allowance, edgestitch along the top edges of the three folds along the second, fourth and sixth lines.

4 Refold the panel and pin or clip along the side edges, to prevent the slots from shifting. Using a ⅛" seam allowance, baste along the side edges. Use a fabric marking pen and ruler to draw a line along the vertical center of the panel. **(J)**

5 Stitch along the line backstitching at the beginning and end.

ASSEMBLING THE ZIPPER POUCH

1 Prepare the 7" zipper by folding the zipper tape on both ends towards the wrong side at a a 45 degree angle. Tack in place. Make sure to stitch only within the seam allowance. **(K)**

2 With the black zipper pocket panel right side up, center the zipper with the teeth side down and the zipper pull on the left. Align the zipper tape with the top edge of the panel and pin or clip to hold in place. Baste, using a ⅛" seam allowance removing the pins as you go.

3 Layer one blue zipper pocket lining panel right side down on the basted zipper panel, aligning all the raw edges. Pin or clip along the top edge (the zipper is sandwiched in between the lining and the main panel). Attach the zipper foot and stitch along the pinned edge using a scant ¼" seam allowance. **(L)**

4 Position the main and the lining panels wrong sides together and press away from the zipper. Repeat for the remaining main and lining panels, sewing them to the opposite side of the zipper tape. **(M)**

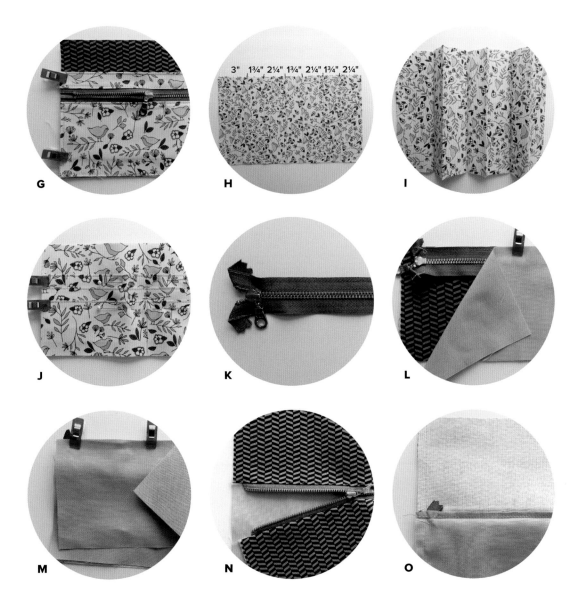

The measurements shown in image H are: 3" 1¾" 2¼" 1¾" 2¼" 1¾" 2¼"

5 Re-attach a regular sewing machine foot. Press the panels away from the zipper. This time, take care to edgestitch on both sides along the zipper using a ⅛" seam allowance through the exterior panels only, not through the lining. Press the linings away from the zipper.

6 Open the zipper about half way **(N)**. Align both the main panels right sides together and the lining panels right sides together. Be sure the seams are pressed towards the main panels. Pin or clip in place, and stitch the side edges only. The bottom edges will remain open. **(O)**

7 Turn the pouch right side out and smooth the lining inside the main pouch. Align the bottom edges and use a ⅛" seam allowance to baste through all the layers along the bottom raw edge.

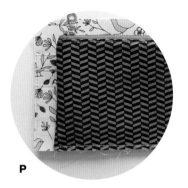
P

Q

R

ASSEMBLING THE CLUTCH LINING

1 With the assembled card slots panel facing right side up on a flat surface, center the assembled zipper pouch on top, aligning the bottom raw edges. Pin or clip in place and use a ⅛" seam allowance to baste through all of the layers. **(P)**

2 With the right sides together, align the assembled lower lining black fabric's top 9" raw edge with the basted edge of the card slots+zipper pouch. Pin or clip in place and stitch along the 9" edge through all of the layers. Press the seam towards the lower lining. Topstitch along the seam on the right side of the lower lining. **(Q)**

3 With the assembled lining facing up on a flat surface, layer the 9" edge of the black flap lining with the top raw edge of the card slots rectangle, right sides together. Pin or clip in place and stitch along the long edge. Press the seam towards the card slots rectangle and edgestitch along that seam on the right side of the card slots rectangle. The fully assembled lining panel should measure 9" wide x 14" tall. Set your lining aside for now. **(R)**

ASSEMBLING THE EXTERIOR

1 With the main exterior panel and exterior flap right sides together, align the 9" raw edges. Clip in place and stitch together. Press the seam towards the main exterior. Topstitch along the seam on the right side of the main exterior.

2 Using a ruler and fabric pen, mark the snap placement 2" away from the bottom and side edges. Follow the manufacturer's directions to attach the male snaps at the marked positions. **(S)**

FINAL ASSEMBLY

1 With the fully assembled exterior and lining panels right sides together, neatly align all the edges and pin or clip all the way around the perimeter. **(T)**

2 Begin stitching along the flap's edge approximately 2" away from the tapered center. Stitch all the way around the perimeter making sure to leave a 4" opening in the flap's top seam, again stopping approximately 2" away from the tapered center.

> **TIP:** It may be helpful to mark the opening in the top flap using two pins as a reminder to leave that 4" opening for turning.

3 Press the open seam around the gap in the flap's top. Clip the corners to reduce the bulk and turn the clutch right side out through the opening.

4 Push out the corners neatly and roll the seams between your fingers to make them neat and flat. Clip to hold the opening in the top seam closed. Edgestitch just along the the flap, with backstitching at the beginning and end and closing the gap in the process. **(U)**

5 Give the clutch a good press using a hot iron with a steam setting.

6 Fold the clutch and use the snap on the exterior to mark the snap placement on the flap. Install the female snaps at the marked positions.

> **TIP:** Take your time installing the female side of the snaps for the perfect fit. First, make sure the edges of the clutch are neatly aligned and that the snaps will not be crooked. Second, don't fold up the clutch too tightly when marking the placement for the snaps. This will leave enough room to be able to close the clutch when it is filled up with all your goodies!

CUSTOMIZATION TIP

Let's talk about creidt card safety for a minute. Since this clutch is designed to house credit cards, you might want to consider adding in a lining of RFDI blocking fabric to your version. These fabrics contain various combinations of metals that can sheild the magnetic cards from radio waves. While there is a good deal of debate on the topic of RFDI theft, the cost to incorporate a layer of this specialty fabric might be worthwhile. If you'd like to add a layer, attach it to the card slot after Step 3 of Assembling the Card Slots (see page 38), before basting the sides together. A variety of suppliers sell these fabrics online. Be sure to follow the manufacturer's instructions with regard to their thread and needle recommendations.

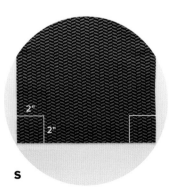

S

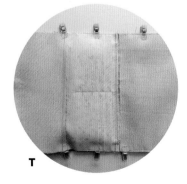

T

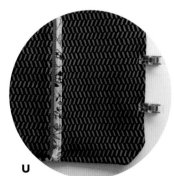

U

OUT-AND-ABOUT CROSSBODY BAG

This is a perfect bag for traveling or running errands. It's just the right size to easily fit all of your essentials plus a few extras. I hope you will love the addition of the front zipper pocket as well as the main zipper closure to keep your treasures safe and secure.

FINISHED SIZE: 10" wide x 9½" tall x 3" deep

SEAM ALLOWANCE: ½" seam allowance unless otherwise noted

MATERIALS

¼ yard floral quilting cotton for main exterior

⅝ yard solid quilting cotton for contrasting exterior bottom + strap

¾ yard quilting cotton for lining

½ yard interlining fabric (canvas or denim)

2 yards medium weight fusible interfacing

(1) 7" zipper

(1) 14" zipper

(2) 1" wide D-rings

(2) 1" wide swivel hooks

(1) 1" wide rectangle strap slider

(4) 6–8mm rivets (optional)

fabric marking pen

small pair of sharp scissors

sewing clips and/or pins

leather hole punch + rivet setting tool (optional)

2 strips of leather for zipper pulls (optional)

CUTTING

Note: *the measurements below are width x height*

From the floral fabric, cut:
(2) 14" x 7½" rectangles for main exterior

From the solid fabric, cut:
(2) 14" x 5" rectangles for contrasting exterior bottom
(2) 14" x 2" strips for lining facings
(2) 33" x 4" strips for straps

(1) 5" x 4" rectangle for D-ring tabs
(1) 1¾" x 3" rectangle for zipper tab

From the lining fabric, cut:
(2) 14" x 10½" rectangles for main lining
(1) 9" x 12" rectangle for exterior zipper pocket
(2) 10" x 5" rectangles for slip pocket

From the interlining, cut:
(2) 14" x 12" rectangles

From the interfacing, cut:
(1) 59" x 4" strip for strap*
(2) 14" x 7½" rectangles for main exterior
(1) 14" x 5" for contrasting exterior bottom
(2) 14" x 2" rectangles for lining facings
(2) 14" x 10½" rectangles for main lining
(1) 10" x 5" rectangle for slip pocket

***Cut this strip for the strap first, along the length of the interfacing.**

PREPARATION

Following the manufacturer's directions, fuse the interfacing to the wrong sides of the main exterior, the contrasting exterior bottom, the lining facings, the main lining and one slip pocket panel.

ASSEMBLING THE STRAP

1 Join the (2) 33" lengths of strap fabric on the diagonal. To do this, position the lengths right sides together at a 90 degree angle. Mark a line on the wrong side of the top strip **(A)**. Sew on this line and trim away the excess, leaving a ¼" seam allowance. Press the seam open and trim to 60" x 4".

2 Center and fuse the 59" strip of interfacing to the wrong side of the strap from Step 1. There will be ½" on each short side without interfacing.

3 Fold and press the short ends of the strap ½" towards the wrong side and press. With the wrong side facing up, fold the strap in half lengthwise and press. Open the strap and align the raw edges to meet in the middle. **(B)**

4 Fold in half again along the first long crease so that the raw edges are encased inside and press.

5 Pin or clip in place to hold the folded edge closed. Edgestitch along all four edges. If desired, stitch a second row of topstitching all the way around the strap using a ¼" seam allowance.

INSTALLING THE D-RING TABS

1 Position the 5" x 4" D-ring tab wrong side up on an ironing surface (please note, no interfacing is adhered to this strip). With the wrong sides together, align the 5" edges together to fold the tab in half lengthwise and press.

2 Open up the tab and, as with the strap, bring the long raw edges towards the middle crease, encasing the raw edges and press. Edgestitch along the two long edges. Repeat using a ¼" seam allowance. Subcut the assembled strip into (2) 2½" long D-ring tabs.

3 Loop a 2½" long tab through the D-ring and fold the tab in half. Clip or pin together to hold both raw edges of the tabs together. Using a ⅛" seam allowance, stitch the raw edges together to form a loop around the D-ring. Repeat to make a second loop + D-ring. Set aside for now. **(C)**

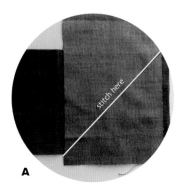

A

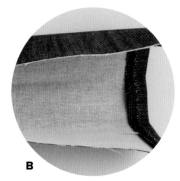

B

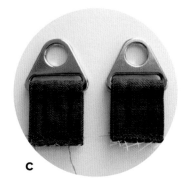

C

ASSEMBLING THE EXTERIOR

1 Using a ¼" seam allowance, attach one exterior bottom panel to a main exterior. Press towards the bottom panel. Edgestitch along the fold on the bottom panel. **(D)**

2 Using a ruler and fabric pen, mark a 1½" square on both corners of the bottom panel. Cut along the drawn lines.

3 Repeat Steps 1–2.

ATTACHING THE EXTERIOR ZIPPER POCKET

1 With the 9" x 12" exterior zipper pocket wrong side up, use a fabric pen and a ruler to mark the zipper opening. To do this, center a 7" line 1" away from the 9" top edge of the pocket. That line will be the top of the rectangle for your zipper opening. Mark a second line ½" away from the first, 1½" away from the top 9" edge of the pocket. Connect the ends of the lines to create a rectangle. Draw a line through the center of the rectangle, and add v-shapes at both ends approximately ¼" away from the short ends of the rectangle.

2 With one assembled exterior panel and the center zipper pocket right sides together, position the top edge of the pocket 2" away from the exterior's top edge, and centered on the exterior panel. The pocket should be 2½" away from either side edge of the exterior. **(E)**

3 Pin the pocket in place and stitch along the drawn rectangle. Using a pair of small sharp scissors, carefully cut through both layers of fabric along the drawn center line and into the v-shapes. Be sure not to cut the stitches.

4 Press the seams open and pull the pocket through the zipper opening to the wrong side of the exterior panel. Finger press to ensure the pocket is as flat as possible, then press with a hot iron so the zipper opening edges are nice and sharp.

> **TIP:** Take your time with this step and use the narrowest tip of your iron to create a neat finish.

5 With the right side of the exterior panel facing up, center the 7" zipper behind the opening with the zipper teeth facing up and the pull on the left. Pin through all the layers and edgestitch around the perimeter of the zipper opening. This will attach the zipper in place and secure the edges of the zipper opening at the same time.

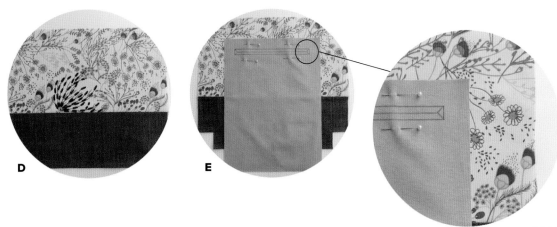

D

E

6 With the exterior panel right side down, align the (2) 9" raw edges of the pocket, right sides facing and aligning all the raw edges **(F)**. Pin in place.

7 Using ¼" seam allowance, sew around the three open sides of the pocket, making sure not to catch the exterior panel in your stitching. Press.

> **TIP:** Gently fold the exterior panel away from the pocket as you stitch. The top edge near the zipper has a narrow seam allowance already, so stitch slowly and take your time.

ASSEMBLING THE EXTERIOR

1 Mark and cut 1½" squares from both bottom corners of the interlining. With an interlining panel and exterior panel wrong sides together, align all the raw edges **(G)**. Baste the panels together. Repeat with the second interlining and exterior panels.

2 With the interlined exterior panels right sides together, align the side and bottom edges, ensuring the horizontal contrasting fabric seams align. Clip in place and stitch along the two sides and the bottom edge leaving the corner cutouts unsewn. Press the seams open.

3 Pinch the bag so one side seam is lined up with the bottom seam and the raw edges of the corner cutouts meet. Pin and stitch along the raw edges using a ¼" seam allowance to box the corner. Repeat for the second corner.

4 Turn the bag exterior right side out. Center one D-ring tab along one side seam of the bag's exterior, aligning the raw edges. Pin to hold in place and baste in place by stitching over the tab a few times going back and forth. Repeat to attach the second D-ring tab to the opposite side and set the assembled bag exterior aside for now. **(H)**

ASSEMBLING THE LINING AND SLIP POCKET

1 Mark and cut away 1½" squares from both bottom corners of the lining panels as you did for exterior panels.

2 Position the two slip pocket rectangles right sides together, aligning the edges. Clip in place and stitch around the perimeter, leaving a 3" opening in one long edge for turning. Clip the corners and press the top seam open. Turn right side out through the opening. Push out the corners using a chopstick or similar blunt object so they are nice and pointy.

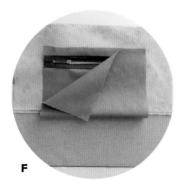

F

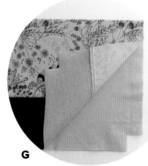

G

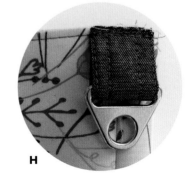

H

3 Press and neatly pin the opening in the top seam closed. Edgestitch along the entire length of the top seam backstitching at the beginning and end. This closes the opening used for turning at the same time. Fold the assembled pocket in half lengthwise and finger press to form a crease. Draw a line through the vertical center of the pocket.

4 Center the finished slip pocket 2" away from the lining's bottom edge and 2¼" away from either side **(I)**. Pin in place to secure and edgestitch around the sides and the bottom, backstitching at the beginning and end. Stitch along the drawn vertical line on the pocket, backstitching at the beginning and end.

PREPARING THE MAIN ZIPPER

1 Fold the tape on the zipper pull end of the 14" zipper towards the wrong side at about a 45 degree angle. Tack in place either by machine or by hand. Stitch only within the seam allowance. **(J)**

2 Place the zipper tab rectangle right side down on your ironing surface, fold both short edges ¼" towards the wrong side and press. Fold the tab in half so the right sides are together and align all the side raw edges. Pin in place and stitch along both side edges using ¼" seam allowance, backstitching at the beginning and end. Clip the corners to reduce the bulk and turn the tab right side out.

3 Position the tab over the end of the zipper tape nearest the zipper stop and pin in place. Using a ⅛" seam allowance, secure the tab to the zipper by stitching along the folded edge of the tab, with backstitching at the beginning and end.

INSTALLING THE MAIN ZIPPER

1 With the assembled lining panel + slip pocket right side up, mark 1½" away from both sides of the lining panel along the top edge. These marks will be used to center the main zipper.

2 Place the 14" zipper with the attached tab right side up along the lining's top edge with one side of the zipper's open tape aligned and pinned at the left 1½" mark. Align the length of one side of the zipper tape with the top lining edge and pin or clip in place. At the second 1½" mark on the right, make a tiny (1/16") snip into the zipper tape and fold down at a 90-degree angle away from the top edge and against the lining. Baste along the length of the pinned zipper between the two marks using a ⅛" seam allowance. **(K)**

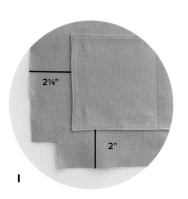

I

J

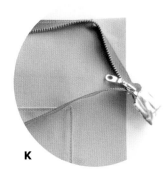

K

3 Install a zipper foot on your machine. Layer one lining facing right side down along the top edge with the zipper sandwiched in between the lining and facing. Clip and stitch along the edge using a ¼" seam allowance. **(L)**

4 Press the seam towards the facing and edgestitch along the fold on the right side of the facing.

5 With the lining panels right sides together, repeat with the second lining panel on the unsewn zipper tape. **(M)**

ASSEMBLING THE LINING

1 With the lining panels still right sides together, align all the edges making sure the horizontal seams of the facing are aligned as well. Tuck the extra length of the tabbed zipper end between the lining panels so it doesn't get caught in the stitches. Clip around the perimeter **(N).** Stitch along the two sides and the bottom edge (but not the notched corners), leaving a 6" opening in the bottom seam for turning.

2 Press the seams open and create the boxed corners referencing Step 3 in Assembling the Exterior (see page 46).

FINAL ASSEMBLY

1 Open the main zipper all the way and insert the assembled exterior of the bag into the lining with the right sides together.

2 Align the side seams as well as the top raw edges of the exterior and the lining. Make sure the D-ring tabs are pushed down and tucked inside. Pin all the way around the top edge of the bag keeping both the raw edges aligned. Stitch all the way around the top edge of the bag.

3 Press the top seam open and turn the bag right side out through the opening in the lining. Stitch the opening in the lining closed and gently push the lining inside the exterior of the bag.

4 Smooth the top edge of the bag with your fingers. Pin through both exterior and lining layers to hold them in place and edgestitch along the top of the bag.

> **TIP:** Sometimes I find it too hard to sew over the sides where the ring tabs are installed, so I usually start and end my stitches where the ring tab is inserted, making sure to backstitch at the beginning and end.

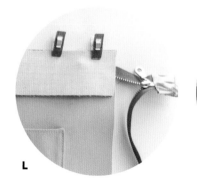

L

M

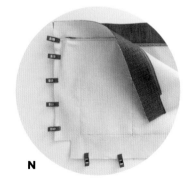

N

ADJUSTABLE STRAP

1 Using a fabric marking pen, mark 1½" away from both short ends of the strap. Thread one end of the strap over the middle bar of the strap slider. Aligning the middle bar with the drawn 1½" mark, align the side edges and clip or pin in place to secure **(O)**. Topstitch two rows of stitching ¼" away from each other, along the edge opposite the hardware.

2 Thread the remaining short end through one swivel hook then through the slider in the area above the attached short end. Bring the end back through the second swivel hook and through the slider in the area below the attached short end **(P)**. Align the bar with the drawn 1½" mark, the align the side edges and clip in place. Topstitch two rows of stitching ¼" away from each other, along the folded edge opposite the hardware. **(Q)**

CUSTOMIZATION TIP

I always look for ways to add a professional-looking finish to my projects. Consider adding rivets to secure both short ends of the bag strap. Attach them through all strap layers ¼" away from each short strap edge **(O)**. Follow the instructions for threading the second strap end through the adjustable strap hardware **(Q)**. Add two additional rivets, as above.

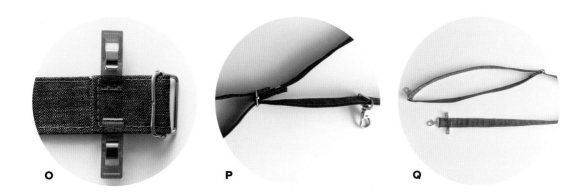

O

P

Q

FRONT ZIPPER POCKET TOTE

This versatile tote with two roomy exterior pockets is sure to make a wonderful companion when running errands, visiting the library, or even going to the beach. I combined Essex linen and a beautiful bold quilting cotton print for the bag exterior which gives the finished tote a fabulously stylish and unique look. I love the addition of leather straps but you can definitely use cotton webbing or make your own fabric straps instead.

FINISHED SIZE: 12" wide x 14" tall x 4" deep

SEAM ALLOWANCE: ½" seam allowance unless otherwise noted

MATERIALS

½ yard medium weight denim, canvas, or Essex linen for main exterior

½ yard quilting cotton for exterior pockets

½ yard quilting cotton for exterior pocket linings

½ yard 54" wide duck canvas, home dec weight fabric, or quilting cotton with a layer of medium-weight fusible interfacing attached for lining

1½ yards medium weight fusible woven interfacing

12" metal or nylon zipper

(1) 18mm magnetic snap

(2) 25" lengths of ¾" wide leather straps

(4) 6mm or 8mm rivets (optional)

fabric marking pen

sharp fabric scissors

leather hole punch & rivet setting tool (optional)

leather for zipper pull (optional)

CUTTING

Note: *measurements are width x height*

From the main exterior fabric, cut:
(1) 13" x 15" rectangle for exterior back
(1) 13" x 4" rectangle for exterior front top
(2) 5" x 15" rectangles for exterior side
(1) 13" x 5" rectangle for exterior bottom
(1) 13" x 2" strip for back pocket binding

From the pocket fabric, cut:
(1) 11" x 13" rectangle for front zipper pocket
(1) 3" x 13" rectangle for front zipper pocket flap
(1) 10½" x 13" rectangle for back slip pocket

From the pocket lining fabric, cut:
(1) 13" x 18" rectangle for front pocket lining
(1) 10½" x 13" rectangle for back pocket lining

From the lining fabric, cut:
(2) 13" x 15" rectangles for main lining
(2) 5" x 15" rectangles for side lining panels
(1) 13" x 5" rectangle for bottom lining panel
(1) 7" x 10" rectangle for slip pocket

From the interfacing, cut:
(1) 13" x 15" rectangle for exterior back
(1) 13" x 4" rectangle for exterior front top
(2) 5" x 15" rectangles for exterior side
(1) 13" x 5" rectangle for exterior bottom
(1) 11" x 13" rectangle for front zipper pocket
(1) 3" x 13" rectangle for front zipper pocket flap
(1) 10½" x 13" rectangle for back slip pocket
(2) 2" squares for magnetic snap reinforcement

PREPARATION

Follow the manufacturer's directions to fuse the interfacing to the wrong side of all the corresponding fabric cuts (except the squares for the magnetic snaps).

ASSEMBLING THE FRONT PANEL

1 With the 11" x 13" front zipper pocket right side up, align the zipper along the top 13" length, with the zipper teeth right side down and the zipper pull on the left. Layer the front pocket lining right side down aligning the top. Pin or clip to hold the layers together. Use a scant ¼" seam allowance to stitch along the pinned edge. **(A)**

> **TIP:** I use a regular presser foot for this step but use a zipper foot if preferred.

2 With the wrong sides together, press the panels away from the zipper and edgestitch along the fold.

3 With the right sides facing, fold up the lining panel aligning the unsewn 13" length with the unsewn edge of the zipper tape. Pin or clip in place and baste along the edge using a ⅛" seam allowance. Baste along the sides and trim away the excess zipper tape. **(B)**

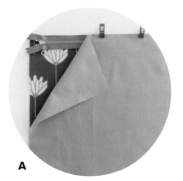
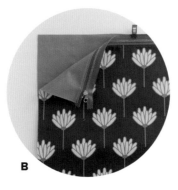

A

B

C

4 With the wrong sides together, fold and press the pocket flap in half lengthwise. With the right sides together, align the raw edges with the top raw edge of the zipper tape. Baste using a ⅛" seam allowance. **(C)**

5 With the exterior front top panel and pocket flap right sides together, align the raw edge. Pin or clip in place and stitch along the edge using a scant ¼" seam allowance. **(D)**

6 Press the top panel away from the pocket and edgestitch along the fold. Set the panel aside for now. **(E)**

Note: The assembled panel should measure 13" wide x 15" long. If yours ended up being a bit longer, just go ahead and trim away the excess fabric along the unsewn edge of the zipper pocket.

ASSEMBLING THE BACK PANEL

1 With the wrong side together, fold the 13" x 2" pocket binding strip in half lengthwise. Press. Open up the strip and press the long raw edges towards the crease. Re-fold in half along the crease, enclosing the long raw edges.

2 With the back slip pocket and back slip pocket lining wrong sides together, align the raw edges. Pin or clip in place and baste the panels together along the top edge using a ⅛" seam allowance.

3 Open the pressed pocket binding and fold over the assembled pocket enclosing the basted edges. Use clips to hold the binding in place. Edgestitch along the length of the binding, attaching the pocket and pocket lining and binding the pocket at the same time. **(F)**

> **TIP:** Go slowly when edgestitching the binding onto the pocket so your stitches look even and as straight as possible.

4 With the right side of the exterior back panel and the pocket lining facing, align the raw edges along the bottom. Pin or clip in place and baste around all three edges using a ⅛" seam allowance. **(G)**

D

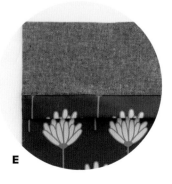

E

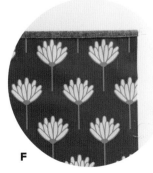

F

ASSEMBLING THE EXTERIOR

1 Use a fabric pen on the wrong side of one side panel and the exterior bottom to mark the stitching line ½" away from the edge, around both of the long and one short edge. This helps accurate stitching.

2 With the front exterior panel and one side panel right sides together, align the long raw edges and clip in place. Beginning at the top of the clipped edge, stitch along the edge, stopping at the marked corner and backstitching **(H)**. Repeat to attach the second side panel to the opposite side of the assembled exterior.

3 Attach both side panels to the back exterior panel using the marked lines as a guide for stitching. Make sure to stop ½" from the bottom edge, backstitching at the beginning and end. The two main panels and two side panels will now form a continuous loop.

4 With the exterior bottom and the front exterior panel right sides together, align the 13" edge of the exterior panel's bottom edge and pin in place. Following the drawn line, stitch together along the length using a ½" seam allowance. Backstitch at the beginning and end.

5 Repeat to attach the unsewn exterior bottom to the remaining back exterior panel as well as the two short ends to the side panels. Press the seams open and clip the corners to reduce the bulk. Turn the exterior right side out.

ATTACHING THE STRAPS

1 Find the middle of the exterior panels by folding them in half and pinching gently along the top edge. Use a fabric marking pen to mark 3" away from each side of the middle point on both the exterior front and exterior back panels.

2 Place one strap right side down along top raw edge of the front exterior panel, aligning the inner edges of the strap with a mark from the previous step. Repeat with the remaining strap end. There will be a 6" gap between the inner edges of the strap. Making sure the strap isn't twisted, pin or clip in place to prevent shifting and baste in place using a ⅛" seam allowance. Repeat to attach the second strap to the back exterior panel.

> **TIP:** If you'd like to add a tag to your tote like I did, just center it 1" up from the front pocket edge and sew in place by hand. **(I)**

G

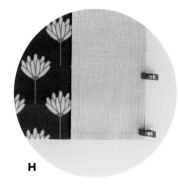

H

I

ASSEMBLING THE INTERIOR SLIP POCKET AND MAGNETIC SNAP

1 With the lining slip pocket right side down, fold and press the 10" top edge ½" towards the wrong side. Repeat to enclose the top raw edge. Edgestitch along the fold.

2 With the wrong sides together, fold and press both side edges and the bottom edge of the slip pocket by ¼".

> **TIP:** If you are a fan of spray starch or spray starch alternative, consider using it here to ensure your folds stay nice and flat.

3 With both right sides up, center the pocket on a main lining panel, 6" away from the top raw edge. Pin and starting at one side edge, edgestitch in place around both sides and the bottom of the pocket. Then stitch again ¼" from the first line of stitching.

4 Use a fabric marking pen and a ruler to make a line 4" away from pocket's left edge (this will be a divider for your pocket). Stitch along the drawn line, backstitching at the beginning and end. **(J)**

5 Center a magnetic snap closure washer 2" away from the panel's top edge. Use a fabric marking pen to mark the exact prong placement and set the washer aside. **(K)**

6 Fuse a 2" square of interfacing on the wrong side of the lining behind the marks for the snap placement.

7 Using a seam ripper or a pair of small, sharp scissors, carefully cut through both layers along the traced lines from Step 5 for the snap prongs. Slide the prongs through from the right side of the lining, place the washer over the prongs and bend the prongs away from each other to secure the snap in place. **(L)**

8 Repeat Steps 5-7 to attach the other snap to the second lining panel without the pocket.

LINING ASSEMBLY

1 Assemble the lining following the same instructions in Assembling the Exterior.

2 Press the seams open, trim them to ¼", then clip the corners to reduce the bulk.

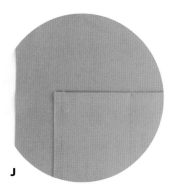

J

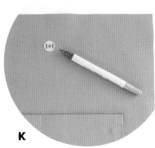

K

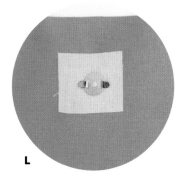

L

FINISHING

1 Insert the assembled exterior into the assembled lining with their right sides together **(M)**. Align the top raw edges as well as the side panel seams of the exterior panel and the lining. Ensure the straps are pushed down and tucked inside the bag away from the top raw edge. Pin or clip all the way around the top edge keeping the raw edges aligned.

2 Stitch all the way around the pinned top edge of the tote using a ½" seam allowance, leaving a 6" opening along the main back panel for turning.

3 Press the top seam open and turn the tote right side out through the opening in the top seam. Gently push the lining inside the exterior. Align the panels and roll the top seam between your fingers to create a crisp edge. Position the straps so they are out of the way of the stitching. Clip around the top of the tote, securing the 6" gap closed as well. **(N)**

4 Edgestitch all the way around the top seam. Press the sewn edge well.

OPTIONAL RIVETS

1 Using a fabric pen, mark ¼" down from the top edge of the exterior centered in the middle of the width of the strap.

2 Following the instructions on page 15, and the manufacturer's instructions, use the setting tool to install a rivet, using the mark from Step 1 as a guide. Be sure to go through all of the layers, including the strap and the lining. **(O)**

3 Repeat for the remaining three straps.

CUSTOMIZATION TIP

Adjust the pockets to suit your desired use for this bag. Need a knitting bag? Create a larger lining pocket rectangle and instead of one divider, add many narrower pockets for storing needles. Need space for a water bottle? Add a simple hemmed rectangle to the side exterior and baste in place along the lower short edge of the side panel before attaching it to the bag exterior. Swim bag? Replace the pocket lining with a laminated fabric for that wet swimming gear.

M

N

O

FOR
YOUR
HOME

BEAR PAW COASTERS

My family has finally reached that glorious stage when all of us actually use coasters without having to be reminded a million times! So, when my kids complained one day that we didn't have enough coasters in the house, I very happily dropped what I was doing and designed these pretties based on the well-known bear paw quilt block. Don't you just love how we makers can do things like that?

This set would make a fabulous house warming or hostess gift too. Just tie a pretty ribbon around them and maybe add a handmade tag and you're good to go.

FINISHED SIZE: 5" square

MATERIALS TO MAKE (2) COASTERS

(1) 4" square of beige or gray fabric

(1) 4" square and (4) 2½" squares of white fabric

(4) 2½" squares of dark blue or yellow fabric

(2) 2" squares of light gray fabric

(2) 6" squares of thin cotton batting

(2) 6" squares of backing fabric (cotton or linen)

(1) 2¼" x WOF strip of fabric for binding

fabric marking pen

clear acrylic ruler

basting pins

hand sewing supplies (optional)

ASSEMBLING THE BLOCK

1 On the wrong side of the 4" white square, draw a diagonal line using a fabric marking pen and a ruler. Position a 4" beige square and the marked white square right sides together and stitch ¼" away on both sides of the drawn line. **(A)**

2 Press to set the stitches and cut along the drawn line. Press the seams towards the darker fabric. Trim the half-square triangle (HST) units to measure 3½" square. **(B)**

3 Repeat with the 2½" squares to create eight HST units. Trim each of these units to measure 2" square. **(C)**

4 Arrange the units as shown to create the bear paw block and piece together. Repeat for the second block. **(D)**

FINISHING

1 With the backing fabric right side down, layer the batting square on top and then the pieced patchwork block right side up. Baste or pin the layers together and quilt as desired. Trim the quilted sandwich to measure 5" square.

> **TIP:** I used sashiko thread and a simple running stitch to hand quilt my coasters.

2 Fold and press the binding strip in half lengthwise with the wrong sides together and press. Attach the binding to your coaster as you would to a quilt. **(E)**

3 Repeat for the second block to create a pair of coasters.

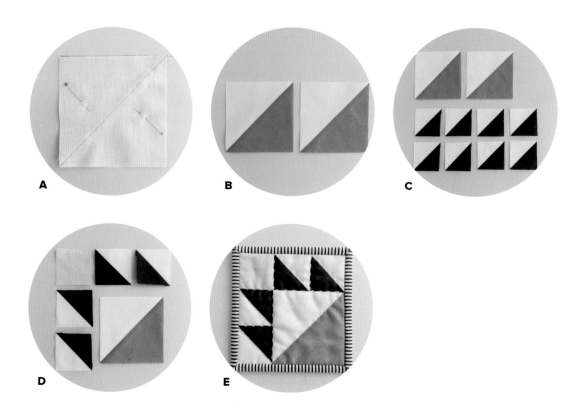

A   B   C

D   E

CUSTOMIZATION TIP

HSTs are such a flexible block. Here are some other simple designs you can use to create a 5" finished coaster. For these designs, you will need to cut 3½" squares from your chosen fabrics. Depending on the design you like, select a balance of focal and background fabrics. Sew the four resulting 2¾" unfinished HSTs into a 4-patch to create the coaster top.

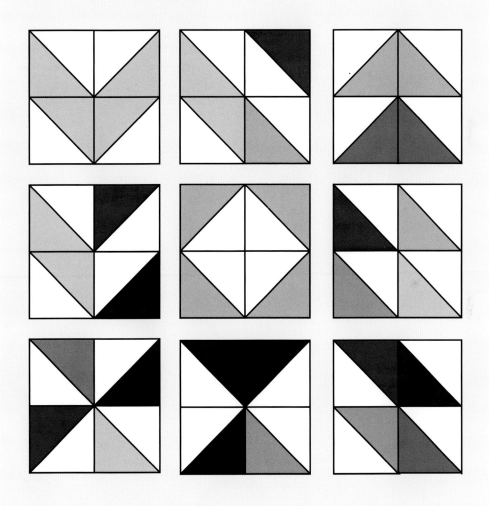

SCRAPPY PLACEMATS

I made these low volume placemats for our kitchen and I just love how they coordinate with each other but are not all matchy — matchy. You can use light colored scraps of fabric just like I did, or you could make each placemat using different colored scraps for a beautiful rainbow effect.

Each placemat finishes at 12" x 15". In my experience they tend to shrink a bit in the first wash so make yours larger if you prefer.

FINISHED SIZE: 12" x 15"

MATERIALS FOR ONE PLACEMAT
enough scrap strips to cover the whole batting plus a few extras (my strips are different lengths and between 1½"–4" wide)

(1) 13" x 16" rectangle of low loft cotton batting

(1) 12" x 15" rectangle of backing fabric

(2) 2¼" x WOF strips for the binding

Note: To create a scrappy binding, stitch some scraps together to give you the desired length of 60".

basting pins

hand stitching supplies (optional)

fabric scissors

INSTRUCTIONS

1 With the batting rectangle on a flat work surface, arrange the scraps in a pleasing manner. Begin in the middle and work in a "log cabin" style by adding more strips around the first scrap in a clockwise pattern until all of the batting is covered. If some of your strips aren't long enough, just add another fabric to make up the desired length. **(A)**

2 Following the Quilt as you Go (QAYG) technique from page 12, begin attaching the fabric to the batting until all of the batting is covered. **(B, C)**

3 Press the patchwork slab well and trim to measure 12" x 15". Using a ⅛" seam allowance, stitch around the perimeter of your placemat to secure the quilting.

4 With the backing and patchwork top wrong sides together, align the raw edges and pin or clip around the perimeter to prevent the layers from shifting. Using a ⅛" seam allowance, baste the two panels together. **(D)**

5 Attach the binding strips on the diagonal to make one continuous strip. Fold and press in half lengthwise and attach the binding to your placemat as you would to a quilt. **(E)**

6 Put a few pins through all of the layers and stitch in the ditch along the seam lines around a few of the rectangles to secure the backing to your placemat.

7 Repeat to make as many more placemats as desired.

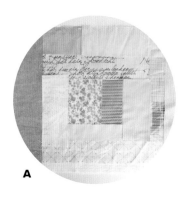

A

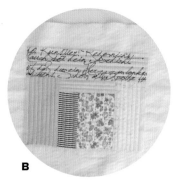

B

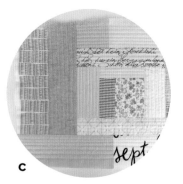

C

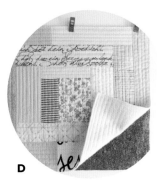

D

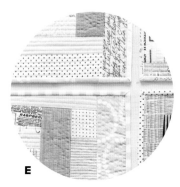

E

CUSTOMIZATION TIP

Did you get hooked on this fast and fun technique? Why not think a little bigger? Create a bunch of 12" squares, stitch them together to form a quilt top, add backing, hand-tie the layers together with a beautiful yarn, and attach your binding as normal.

Or maybe think smaller! Swap out a pieced QAYG panel for any of the exterior panels listed in the projects in this book. Below are pictures of some projects I have made over the years using this scrap-buster method of piecing. The coasters in the previous project would make a lovely housewarming gift when paired with a bunch of placemats. Need a quick gift? Make a small QAYG square to be the top of a pincushion. Endless quilty possibilities....

BOXY FLOOR CUSHION

Floor cushions are a great way to add not just extra seating, but also a bit of color, pattern, and personality to just about any room. And you don't have to stop at making just one. Make an entire stack of these to have on hand when unexpected guests suddenly arrive.

FINISHED SIZE: 18" square x 2½" deep

MATERIALS

Note: *the measurements below are width x height*

fabric A: (1) 5½" x 13" rectangle

fabric B: (1) 9" x 6" rectangle

fabric C: (1) 9" x 7½" rectangle

fabric D: (1) 8" x 13" rectangle

fabric E: (1) 9" square

fabric F: (1) 8" x 5" rectangle

fabric G: (1) 5½" x 5" rectangle

fabric H: (1) 13" x 4½" rectangle

(1) 21½" square of fusible fleece

(1) 21½" square of backing fabric (canvas or linen)

(1) 20" length of yarn or strong thread

20 oz bag of polyfilll

tapestry needle

fabric marking pen

ruler

fabric scissors

ASSEMBLING THE PILLOW

1 Piece together the fabric B and C rectangles along the 9" edge. Press the seam to one side. Add the fabric A rectangle to the left side and fabric D rectangle to the right side of the B/C panel. Set the panel aside.

2 Piece together the fabric F and G rectangles along the 5" edge. Press the seam to one side. Add the fabric H rectangle to the bottom seam, then add the fabric E square on the left.

3 Attach both panels together along the length and press well. The pillow top should measure 21½" x 21½". **(A)**

4 Following the manufacturer's instructions, fuse the assembled pillow panel to the fusible fleece.

5 Locate the middle of your pillow top by folding it in half diagonally and then diagonally again. The middle point is where the folds meet. Use the fabric marking pen to mark the middle point on the right side of the fabric. Repeat for the backing as well.

6 With the assembled pillow top and backing right sides together, align all the raw edges and pin or clip in place to prevent the layers from shifting. Using a ½" seam allowance, stitch around the perimeter leaving a 7" opening in the bottom seam. Backstitch at the beginning and end.

7 Press open the bottom seam (the one with the opening for turning).

8 Place the assembled pillow on a flat work surface. Using a fabric pen and a clear ruler to mark a 1¼" square on each corner. Cut away the squares. **(B)**

9 Reach into the pillow through the hole in the bottom seam, flatten the side seams over each other and stitch along the folded seam to box the corner. Repeat for the remaining three corners. **(C)**

10 Turn the pillow right side out through the opening and gently stuff with polyfilll adding a bit at a time until it's nice and fluffy but not overstuffed. The pillow should have more of a boxy, rectangular shape, and not be too rounded.

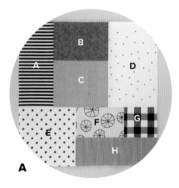

A

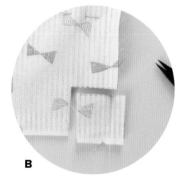

B

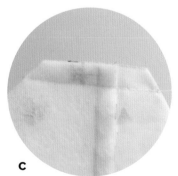

C

11 Neatly fold the edges of the opening inside the pillow, line them up on top of each other and clip the opening closed. Sew the gap closed either by machine or by hand. **(D)**

ADDING THE TUFT

1 Thread the length of yarn through the tapestry needle. Slowly push the needle into the pillow at the middle mark of the pillow top and coming out on the backing at the middle mark again.

> **TIP:** Adding the tuft can be a bit tricky as the pillow is probably thicker than your needle. Squish the pillow as much as you need to when getting the needle to the other side.

2 Place the needle ¼" away from the previous stitch and bring the needle up through the backing, coming out on the front about ¼" away from the first stitch. Repeat one more time. **(E)**

3 Both the yarn ends will be poking through the pillow top. Pull on these ends to tuft the pillow as much as you like. Double knot the yarn together and trim the excess ends to ½". **(F)**

CUSTOMIZATION TIP

Adding a custom fabric label can be a lovely way to personalize any project, especially if it is a gift. You can find small businesses on etsy.com and search 'custom fabric labels' to find quite a few shops selling label printing services. Most offer fabric labels of many styles, fonts and substrates– even leather–for around $20 a batch. These quickly add that handmade touch to any project.

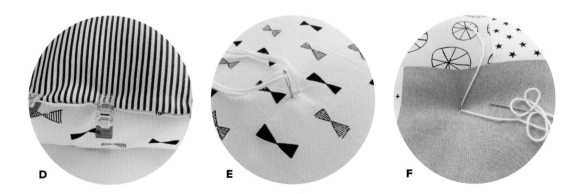

D

E

F

BIG STITCH THROW PILLOWS

A piece of linen, some lovely sashiko thread and a bit of patience is all you need to make these stylish throw pillows. Don't worry if your stitches look a bit wobbly at the beginning. Just relax and keep stitching. The more you practice, the prettier and more even your stitches will get.

FINISHED SIZE: 17" square

SEAM ALLOWANCE: ½" unless otherwise noted

MATERIALS

(1) 18" square of quilting cotton or linen for pillow front

(1) 18" square of fusible fleece

(1) 18" wide x 19" tall rectangle of quilting cotton or linen for pillow back

(1) 18" wide x 2½" tall rectangle of quilting cotton or linen for contrasting zipper flap

(1) 20" nylon zipper

(1) 18" pillow form

sashiko sewing supplies (sashiko thread, needle and thimble)

tracing tools (tracing paper and a tracing wheel)

sewing machine zipper foot

EMBELLISHING THE PILLOW FRONT

1 Fuse the fleece to the wrong side of the pillow front following the manufacturer's directions. Using a zig zag or overlock stitch, sew around the perimeter to prevent the edges from fraying.

2 Using a pattern on page 124 or 125, trace the stitching pattern onto the right side of the pillow front.

3 Knotting the end of the sashiko thread, begin stitching by pulling the needle through from the wrong side of the front panel to ensure that the knot secures the thread on the wrong side. Using a running stitch, make neat and even stitches along the marked lines, again making a small knot on the wrong side when finished. **(A)**

ASSEMBLING THE PILLOW BACK

1 Subcut the pillow back rectangle into (1) 8" tall x 18" wide and (1) 11" tall x 18" wide rectangle.

2 Using a zig zag or overlock stitch, stitch around the perimeter of both pillow back panels as well as the zipper flap to prevent the edges from fraying.

3 With the subcut 11" x 18" backing panel from Step 1 right side up on a flat work surface, position the zipper right side down along an 18" edge, aligning the raw edges. Pin or clip in place and install the zipper foot on your machine. Using a scant ¼" seam allowance, attach the zipper to the panel. **(B)**

4 Press the backing fabric away from the zipper and edgestitch along the fold for a neat finish.

5 Fold the zipper flap in half lengthwise with the wrong sides facing and press. Align the raw edges with the unsewn zipper tape, ensuring the side edges align with the back panel. Pin or clip in place and baste together using a ⅛" seam allowance. **(C)**

6 Layer the subcut 8" x 18" back panel from Step 1 right side down along the basted zipper tape. Pin or clip in place and stitch through all of the layers using a scant ¼" seam allowance. **(D)**

7 Press the 8" back panel away from both the zipper and the zipper flap. Press and edgestitch along the fold on the right side of the back panel.

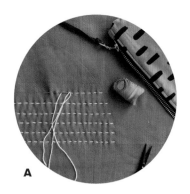

A

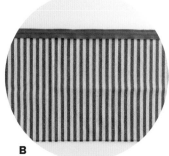

B

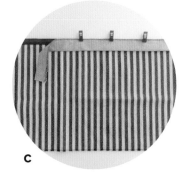

C

8 Open the zipper about half way. Make a few back and forth stitches along both side edges along the short edges of the zipper flap, making sure the zipper pull is under the flap. Trim away the excess zipper tape from both sides.

9 If necessary, trim away any excess fabric along the bottom edge of the panel so that it measures 18" square. To prevent fraying, be sure to go back and finish the newly trimmed edge with a zigzag or overlock stitch if necessary. **(E)**

FINISHING

1 With the front and back panels right sides together, pin or clip around the perimeter to hold both panels together. Stitch all the way around the perimeter, then turn the pillow cover right side out. Gently push the corners out to make them neat and pointy.

2 Neatly stuff the form inside the finished pillow case. Zip up the cover and enjoy!

CUSTOMIZATION TIP

Sashiko thread is a thick cotton thread that isn't made in separate strands like embroidery floss. It also tends to have a natural matte finish unlike the sheen some embroidery flosses have. If Sashiko threads and needles are hard to find, feel free to substitute in a different thread or floss for this project. The finished look will be different though, so bear that in mind.

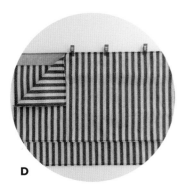

D

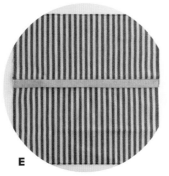

E

PUFFY DUVET

This super-squishy and comfy classic patchwork duvet would make a great baby shower, birthday or even a housewarming present. It's quick and surprisingly easy to make. You could definitely complete one in a weekend if you set your mind to it.

My fabric requirements yield a throw-sized duvet. You can, however, make it a bit smaller or larger depending on your needs. Just use fewer or more blocks to make your patchwork and adjust the size of the batting and backing accordingly.

FINISHED SIZE: 51" x 66"

SEAM ALLOWANCE: ½" unless otherwise noted

MATERIALS
20 fat quarters of quilting cotton

52" x 68" high loft polyester batting (I used ¾" loft polyester batting)

4 yards of fabric for backing

yarn for tying

tapestry needle

painters/masking tape (optional)

basting spray

fabric scissors

sewing machine walking foot attachment (optional)

hand sewing supplies (optional)

fabric marking pen

hand sewing needle with a large enough eye to accomodate your yarn

ASSEMBLING THE DUVET TOP

1 Cut (2) 11" wide x 9" tall rectangles from each fat quarter for a total of forty (40) rectangles. Arrange the rectangles into a 5 x 8 grid to create the patchwork top. **(A)**

2 Assemble the duvet top by stitching the rectangles into eight rows and then stitching the rows together.

> **TIP:** Press the seams on each even row to the left side and each odd row to the right side so the seams nest nicely during the final assembly.

3 Press the assembled duvet top to get rid of all the wrinkles.

4 Following the manufacturer's instructions and working in a well-ventilated room or outside, spray both the batting and back of the duvet top with basting spray to help with adhesion. This is especially important when using polyester batting since it does not seem to naturally adhere well to the cotton fabric. But for this project, I like to use the polyester for the extra loft.

> **TIP:** Shake the basting spray can vigorously for a few minutes before starting to spray. This prevents any glue stains forming on your fabric.

5 Layer the assembled duvet patchwork top on top of the batting, with the sprayed sides together. Smooth out any wrinkles.

6 Use scissors to trim the batting to the exact size of the duvet top and set aside.

7 Cut the backing fabric into two equal lengths and remove the selvages. Stitch the two pieces together along the long edge. Press the seam open.

8 With the backing right side up on a flat surface, smooth it making sure there are no creases or puckers. Use painter's tape to keep the backing nice and smooth if working on a hardwood floor. Position the basted duvet top and the backing right sides together. The batting is now facing up and will be smaller than the backing fabric. Ensure all of the layers are nice and flat, but don't stretch it too much otherwise the layers may shift and distort the rectangular shape. Pin around the perimeter through all the layers (be generous with your pins). **(B)**

9 If you have one, install a walking foot on your machine. Stitch around the perimeter, leaving a 10" opening in one of the sides for turning. Backstitch at the beginning and end of your stitching. **(C)**

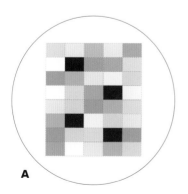

A

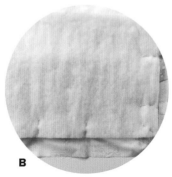

B

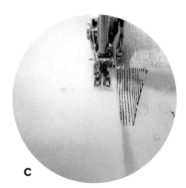

C

10 Trim the backing to the size of the duvet top and batting. Clip the corners to reduce the bulk being careful not to cut through any stitching. Turn the duvet right side out through the 10" gap from Step 9. Push the corners out to make them nice and pointy and roll the side seams between your fingers to neatly align them.

> **TIP:** Give the duvet a light press to help with setting the seams, but be very careful not to use an iron that's too hot as it can melt the batting.

11 Use pins or clips to hold the gap closed and stitch shut either by hand or machine.

12 Smooth the duvet neatly over a flat surface making sure all of the layers are spread evenly without any puckers on the top or on the backing. At this point, the backing should be sticking to the batting quite nicely all on its own which prevents the need for any more basting of the layers prior to tying. If, however, it seems that the layers are shifting, loosely pin and baste the duvet through all of the layers.

13 Tie the duvet in the center of each point where four rectangles meet. To do this, thread a tapestry needle with a length of yarn. Work from the front side to the back and take a stitch ¼" away from the fabric intersection where the tie will be knotted **(D)**. Clip the yarn leaving approximately a 3" length on each and tie in a double knot. Trim the remaining yarn ends to the desired length. **(E)**

14 Refer to the quilt spacing information on your batting packaging to determine the distance between the tie placements and repeat to add additional ties through all the layers. **(F)**

CUSTOMIZATION TIP

Be sure to explore different batting options suitable for this project. If you normally prefer a low-loft batting for quilt making, selecting a high loft can feel unusual; however, it will provide the luxurious puffiness this project requires. Check the batting packaging to confirm the minimum quilting distance required and adjust the distance between your ties accordingly.

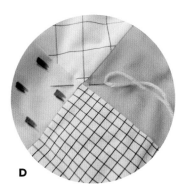

D

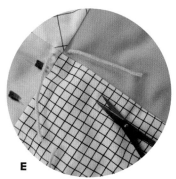

E

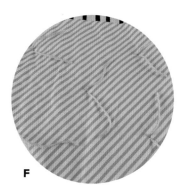

F

RED AND WHITE QUILT

The Sawtooth Star block is one of my all-time favorite quilting blocks. I love that it's been around for ages, yet it looks surprisingly fresh and modern. I guess certain things just never go out of style.

I've always greatly admired beautiful red and white vintage quilts so I decided to make my stars in red solid fabric and float them on a sea of white with a tiny bit of low volume prints sprinkled around.

FINISHED SIZE: 53" x 61"

MATERIALS
Note: yardage based on 42" wide fabric

½ yard of red fabric

3¼ yards of white fabric

4 yards of backing fabric

½ yard of binding fabric

(1) 60" x 70" rectangle of batting

CUTTING
From the red fabric, cut:
(5) 2½" x WOF strips
   subcut into:
      (80) 2½" squares

From the white fabric, cut:
(3) 4½" x WOF strips
   subcut into:
      (20) 4½" squares
(2) 3½" x WOF strips
   subcut into:
      (20) 3½" squares

(4) 2" x WOF strips
   subcut into:
      (80) 2" squares
(9) 2½" x WOF strips
   subcut into:
      (20) 2½" x 6½" rectangles
      (20) 2½" x 8½" rectangles
(5) 11" x WOF strips for borders

From the binding fabric, cut:
(6) 2½" x WOF strips

Tip: Add a bit more interest and movement by substituting out a few of the white rectangles with low volume prints instead (see the grey rectangles in the illustration below).

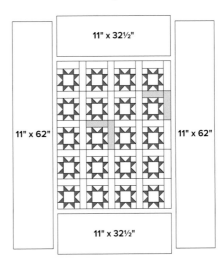

11" x 32½"

11" x 62"

11" x 62"

11" x 32½"

TO MAKE ONE BLOCK, GATHER:
(4) 2½" red squares, (1) 4½" white square
(1) 3½" white square, (4) 2" white squares

ASSEMBLING THE FLYING GEESE
1 On the wrong side of the 2½" red squares, draw a diagonal line. **(A)**

2 With a 4½" white square right side up, position two red squares right side down aligning the raw edges in opposite corners of the 4½" square (the red squares will overlap slightly in the middle). Pin the squares in place. Using a scant ¼" seam allowance, stitch along both sides of the drawn lines across both red squares. Press to set the seams. **(B)**

3 Cut the unit along the drawn line from Step 2 **(C)**. Press the seams towards the red triangles. **(D)**

4 With the right sides together, align another 2½" red square with the raw edges of the assembled unit making sure the drawn line goes between the two red triangles. Pin in place. Using a scant ¼" seam allowance, stitch along both sides of the drawn line. Repeat for the second assembled unit. **(E)**

5 Set the seams and cut the units along the drawn lines **(F)**. Press the seams towards the red triangles and trim each of the flying geese units to 2" x 3½". **(G)**

ASSEMBLING THE BLOCKS
1 Using the remaining white squares and the assembled flying geese units, arrange the block into three rows to create the star shape. **(H)**

2 Stitch the units together into three rows. Press the seams away from the geese. Stitch the rows together. Press.

3 Repeat to create (20) 6½" star blocks.

4 With the right sides together and aligning the raw edges, attach a 2½" x 6½" white (or low volume print) rectangle along the top of each star block. Press the seams away from the stars.

5 Repeat Step 4 to attach a 2½" x 8½" white (or low volume print) rectangle along the right edge of each star block. Press the seams away from the stars. **(I)**

ASSEMBLING THE QUILT TOP
1 Referencing the illustration on page 81, arrange the blocks in 5 rows of 4 blocks each. With the right sides facing and aligning the raw edges, stitch together the blocks in each row. Press the seams in opposite directions every other row.

2 Stitch the rows together, nesting the seams, and press.

3 Remove the selvage from the white border strips. Cut one WOF strip in half along the width. With the right sides together, attach them to two WOF strips along the 11" sides and press. This will yeild (2) 11" x 62½" rectangles. Trim the remaining two WOF strips to 11" x 32½".

4 With the right sides together, stitch a 32½" long border to the top and the bottom of the assembled unit from Step 2 and press the seams. Repeat to attach a 62½" long border to both sides. Give the completed top a good press.

FINISHING
1 Cut the backing fabric into two equal lengths and remove the selvage. Stitch the two pieces together along the long edge using a ½" seam allowance. Press the seam open.

2 Make a quilt sandwich by layering the quilt top, batting and backing. Baste and quilt using your preferred method (I spray basted my quilt and hand quilted it in a simple grid pattern).

3 Trim the backing and batting to match the quilt top's size. Bind using your favorite method.

CUSTOMIZATION TIP

Use a single block to dress up the front panel of the cross-body bag or drawstring tote. Simply create a single block, and then add background fabric to create the exterior panel of the required size.

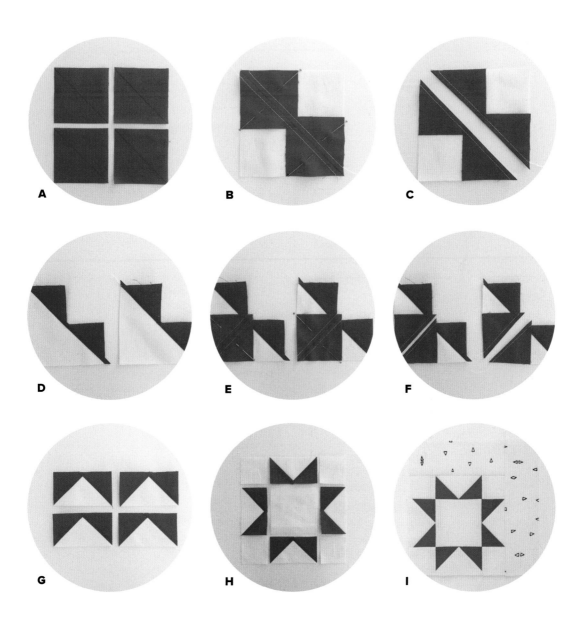

FOR
YOUR
CRAFT
SPACE

WALL POCKET

Out of sight, out of mind — that's me in a nutshell when it comes to many small items that I need on a regular basis but can never, ever find when needed. So, I designed these wall pockets to help me stay organized. I have a few of them hanging from wall hooks in my studio and I'm totally in love.

FINISHED SIZE: 6" wide x 7" tall x 3" deep

MATERIALS

1 fat quarter of quilting cotton or linen for exterior

1 fat quarter of quilting cotton for lining

½ yard of medium weight fusible interfacing

(1) 9½" length of ¾" wide leather for handle

fabric marking pen

fabric scissors

ruler

decorative tag, rivets and leather hole punch (optional)

CUTTING

From the exterior fabric and lining fabric, cut:
(2) 9½" wide x 9" tall rectangles

From the interfacing, cut:
(4) 9½" wide x 9" tall rectangles

PREPARATION

1 Fuse the interfacing to the wrong sides of all of the fabric cuts.

2 Using a fabric marking pen and a ruler, mark a 1½" square on the right side of an exterior rectangle along the two bottom corners. Using a sharp pair of fabric scissors, cut away the corner squares along the drawn lines. **(A)**

3 Repeat for the second exterior rectangle as well as both lining rectangles. **(B)**

ASSEMBLING THE EXTERIOR AND LINING

1 With the right sides together, align the raw edges of the two exterior rectangles and pin or clip along both sides and the bottom edge. Stitch along the pinned edges backstitching at the beginning and end, leaving the corner cutouts unsewn. **(C)**

2 Repeat with the two lining rectangles but leave a 3" opening in the bottom seam for turning.

3 Box the corners by reaching inside the exterior and aligning one side seam over the bottom seam. Pin or clip in place and stitch along the opening. Repeat for the second exterior and the two lining corners. **(D)**

ATTACHING THE HANDLE

1 Fold the back exterior panel's top edge in half and pinch gently to create a crease in the middle. Using a fabric marking pen and a ruler, mark 1¾" away from each side of the crease. Position the strap right side up along the right side of the back exterior panel, aligning the raw edges. The inner edges of the handle should be placed at the 1¾" marks (there will be a 3½" gap between the inner edges of the handle). Make sure not to twist the handle before clipping it in place. **(E)**

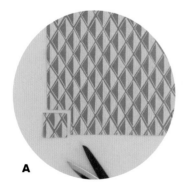
A

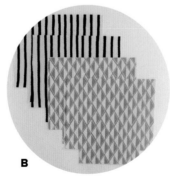
B

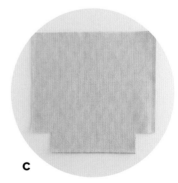
C

2 Baste the handle in place, going back and forth a few times to secure it.

TIP: I recommend using a 90/14 or leather sewing machine needle and polyester thread when working with leather handles. Sew slowly and line everything up before you stitch.

FINISHING

1 Insert the exterior into the lining with the right sides facing. Clip around the top of the bag and stitch around the pinned edge. Turn right side out through the opening in the lining. Stitch the gap in the lining closed and gently push it inside.

2 Smooth the pocket's top edge with your fingers (roll the seam between your fingers to make it lay neat and flat). Use clips to keep the top seam lined up and edgestitch around the circumference. Stitch again, ¼" away from the previous stitches for a decorative finish. **(F)**

CUSTOMIZATION TIP

Create you own or purchase leather labels to add that handmade touch. To install a leather label with rivets, follow the instructions below.

1 Use a leather hole punch to creates hols in the label. Center the decorative label on the front exterior, 1½" away from the top edge. Using a fabric marking pen, mark the rivet placement.

2 Use a leather hole punch to create holes through just the front panels of both the exterior and the lining.

3 Following the manufacturer's instructions, install the rivets to hold your label securely in place.

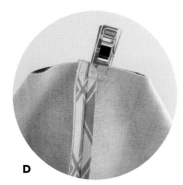

D

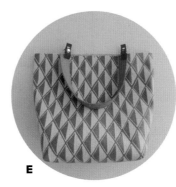

E

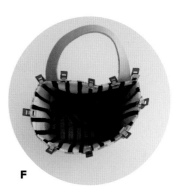

F

PYRAMID PINCUSHION

A good, sturdy pincushion is a must for a well-organized sewing space. These fun pyramid shaped pincushions are surprisingly quick and easy to make. All you need is a piece of your favorite fabric, a cup of rice, and an optional ribbon and you'll be able to whip up this cutie in no time.

FINISHED SIZE: 4" wide x 3½" tall x 4½" deep

MATERIALS

(1) 9" x 5" rectangle quilting cotton

(1) 9" x 5" rectangle medium weight fusible interfacing

(1) 2½" length of ¾" wide thin leather or ribbon

approx. 1 cup rice or crushed walnut shells

small amount of polyfill

funnel

point turner

hand sewing supplies and coordinating thread

ASSEMBLING THE PINCUSHION

1 Fuse the interfacing to the wrong side of the quilting cotton.

2 Fold the leather or ribbon in half. Align the short edges and position these along the cotton rectangle's top edge, 3½" from the right side edge. Baste in place using a ⅛" seam allowance. **(A)**

3 Fold the assembled panel in half with the right sides facing, aligning the short edges. With the fold at the left, stitch along the top and right edge leaving a 1½" opening in the top seam for turning and backstitching at the beginning and end. Clip the corners to reduce the bulk. **(B)**

4 Press the seams open and form the panel into a pyramid shape by moving the right edge's seam to the center of the bottom edge. Pin or clip in place to hold the layers together. **(C)**

5 Stitch along the bottom seam backstitching at the beginning and end. Trim the corners to reduce the bulk.

6 Turn the pincushion right side out through the opening. Push the corners out to make them neat and pointy (use a point turner or similar blunt object for this step).

7 Using the funnel, fill the pincushion with the rice or crushed walnut shells. Add polyfilll to completely stuff your pincushion.

8 With the wrong sides together, neatly fold in the raw edges of the opening inside the pincushion. Pin or clip in place and hand stitch the opening closed.

CUSTOMIZATION TIP

This pattern is perfect for making pattern weights as well. Modify the size by cutting the fabric and interfacing to 5" x 3". Skip adding the ribbon or leather tab and fill entirely with rice. Follow the directions for Pyramid Pincushion to make as many of these fun and useful pattern weights as you wish.

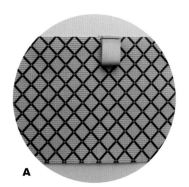

A

B

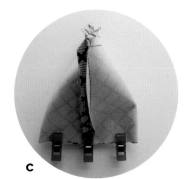

C

WIP POUCH

These generously sized pouches with their see-through vinyl fronts are perfect to keep WIPS (works in progress) organized. I used to be quite intimidated by the idea of sewing with vinyl, thinking it was too fussy and difficult to work with. Once I gave it a try, I was pleasantly surprised. Pay a bit more attention to avoid damaging the vinyl during the assembly process by following my TIPS on the next page. The finished result is worth a bit of extra effort.

FINISHED SIZE: 10" x 11"

MATERIALS

⅓ yard of quilting cotton for the pouch

⅛ yard of quilting cotton for the binding

⅓ yard of vinyl

(1) 11" x 12" rectangle of low-loft cotton batting

(1) 12" or longer nylon zipper

basting pins

fabric marking pen + ruler

sewing clips

utility scissors

hand sewing supplies

CUTTING

From the quilting cotton, cut:

(2) 11" x 12" rectangles for the quilted back panel

(2) 2" x 10" strips for the zipper binding

(1) 2½" x 42" strip for the pouch binding

From the vinyl, cut:

(1) 10" x 9" rectangle

(1) 10" x 2" rectangle

TIPS FOR SEWING WITH VINYL

- I had no issues using a metal presser foot when I worked on my pouch. If your machine is giving you a hard time try a Teflon presser foot instead.

- Use sewing clips (not pins) and attach the clips within the seam allowance to prevent damage to the vinyl.

- Don't use an iron on vinyl. Finger press or use a seam roller instead.

- If there are fold marks in your vinyl, smooth and stretch it out and place a few heavy books on top for a few hours to straighten them out.

ASSEMBLING THE BACK PANEL

1 Make a quilt sandwich by layering an 11" x 12" fabric panel right side down, then add the cotton batting, then the second 11" x 12" fabric panel right side up. Use basting pins to hold the layers together. Mark and quilt the panel (I quilted my panel in a random grid pattern).

2 Press well and trim the quilted back panel to 10" wide x 11" tall. Baste around the perimeter to prevent the quilting stitches from coming undone. Set the back panel aside for a while.

ASSEMBLING THE FRONT PANEL

1 Fold a 2" x 10" zipper binding strip in half lengthwise and press. Open the strip, bring the long raw edges towards the middle crease and press. Re-fold the strip, enclosing both long raw edges. Repeat with the second binding strip.

2 Open one binding strip from Step 1 and place it over a 10" edge of a vinyl rectangle. The vinyl should be snug against the fold of the binding strip. Clip the strip in place and edgestitch along the lower folded edges of the binding strip through all the layers. Repeat for the second binding strip and vinyl rectangle.

TIP: Edgestitch slowly to prevent the binding from bunching up.

3 Using a fabric marking pen and a ruler, clearly mark on the right side of the zipper tape the 10" area where the vinyl panels will be attached. **(A)**

4 Open the zipper all the way. Using the drawn lines from Step 3 as a guide, center the smaller assembled rectangle along the top of the zipper tape edge with the folded edge of the binding closest to the zipper teeth. Clip the layers together. Stitch the zipper in place. **(B)**

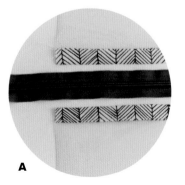

A

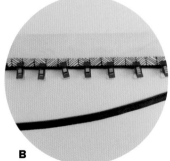

B

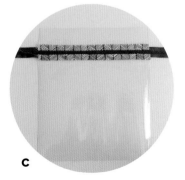

C

TIP: In order to allow the zipper to close smoothly, don't bring the binding all the way to the zipper teeth. Leave about ⅛" of zipper tape exposed between the zipper teeth and fabric.

5 Repeat to attach the second assembled rectangle to the opposite zipper tape. **(C)**

6 Open the zipper about ¼ of the way, sew a few rows of stitches along both short ends of the zipper within the binding strips to secure the edges. Trim away any excess zipper tape. **(D)**

7 Trim the assembled front panel along the bottom edge so the panel measures 10" wide x 11" tall.

FINISHING

1 With the quilted back panel right side up, layer the front vinyl panel also right side up aligning all the edges. If the panels are slightly different sizes, trim along the bottom edge to bring them to the same size. Use clips to hold the panels in place and baste around the perimeter. **(E)**

2 Fold and press the remaining binding strip in half lengthwise. Attach the binding as you would to a quilt. **(F)**

CUSTOMIZATION TIP

Easily adjust the size of this bag to suit whatever project you might be working on. Have 12" quilt blocks that you would like to keep together? Increase the cut size of the rectangles and the length of the binding strips and the zipper and you are all set! Need a pencil pouch for school? Shorten the length and even add in a set of grommets to allow the pouch to fit nicely in a three-ring binder.

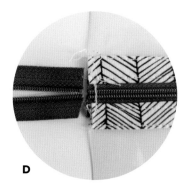

D

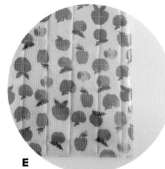

E

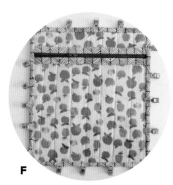

F

ON-THE-GO PROJECT BAG

I love having a knitting project (or two) when we travel or when I'm waiting at the doctor's office or in the carpool lane waiting to pick my kids up from school. I designed this drawstring bag to be just the right size to fit in most of the supplies I might need for an on-the-go project. Whether you like knitting, crochet, or hand sewing, just fill up this handy bag and it will be ready for when you need to run out the door.

FINISHED SIZE: 10" wide x 12" tall x 4" deep

SEAM ALLOWANCE: ½" unless otherwise noted

MATERIALS

1 fat quarter of quilting cotton for main exterior

1 fat quarter of quilting cotton for contrasting exterior bottom + drawstring casing

½ yard canvas or home dec for lining + slip pocket

(2) 14" lengths of ¾" wide leather strips for handles

(2) 36" lengths of ½" wide ribbon or cording

½ yard medium weight fusible interfacing

large safety pin or bodkin

fabric marking pen and ruler

CUTTING

Note: *measurements are width x height*

From the main exterior fabric, cut:
(2) 15" x 9" rectangles for main exterior panels

From the contrasting exterior fabric, cut:
(2) 15" x 6" rectangles for contrasting exterior bottom panels
(2) 15" x 2" strips for drawstring casing

From the lining fabric, cut:
(2) 15" x 14" rectangles for lining
(1) 10" x 7" rectangle for slip pocket

From the interfacing, cut:
(2) 15" x 9" rectangles for main exterior panels
(2) 15" x 6" rectangles for contrasting exterior bottom panels

PREPARATION

Following the manufacturer's instructions, fuse the interfacing to the wrong sides of both the main exterior panels and the contrasting exterior bottom panels.

PREPARING THE CASING

1 With the wrong sides facing, fold both short edges of a casing strip to the wrong side by ¼". Press, then fold another ¼" to enclose the raw edges. Press and stitch along the edges using a ⅛" seam allowance. Fold the casing in half lengthwise and press again. **(A)**

2 Repeat with the remaining casing strip.

ASSEMBLING THE EXTERIOR PANELS

1 With the right sides together and aligning the raw edges, stitch a contrasting rectangle to the bottom of the main panel along the 15" edge. Press the seam towards the contrasting bottom panel.

2 On the contrasting fabric, topstitch along the fold and sew a second line of topstitching ¼" away from the first. Repeat for the second main panel and contrasting rectangle. **(B)**

ATTACHING THE HANDLES

1 Fold one assembled exterior panel in half along the 15" edge and pinch it gently to create a crease at the top. Mark near the top raw edge, 2½" away from the crease on both sides.

2 Position one leather handle right side down along the raw top edge and with the inner edges of the handle aligned with the 2½" marks (there should be a 5" gap between the inner edges of the handle). Make sure not to twist the handle.

3 Baste the handle in place using a ⅛" seam allowance, going back and forth a few times to properly secure it.

4 Align the raw edges of one prepared casing with the top raw edge of the exterior panel, so that the handle is sandwiched between them and the casing is centered (the casing will end about ½" away from each long side of the exterior panel). Ensure the handle is still lying straight and not at an angle. Clip all of the layers in place and baste along the casing to attach it to exterior panel using a ⅛" seam allowance. **(C)**

5 Repeat for the second assembled exterior panel, leather handle and prepared casing.

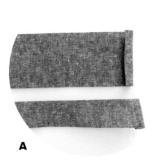

A

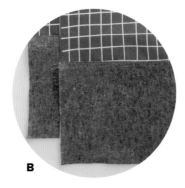

B

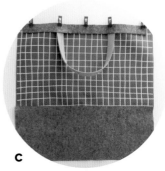

C

ASSEMBLING THE EXTERIOR

1 With the two assembled exterior panels right sides together, align the raw edges and stitch along the bottom edge only. Press the seam open.

2 Using a fabric marking pen and a ruler, mark a horizontal line on the wrong side of an exterior panel, 2½" away from the bottom sewn edge from Step 1. Repeat on the other side of the assembled exterior on the wrong side. **(D)**

3 Fold in both exterior panels right sides together along the 2½" drawn lines. The bottom seam will now be between the right sides of the exterior panels **(E)**. Pin or clip along both long sides of the exterior to prevent shifting. Be sure to align the vertical seams of the contrasting fabric as you clip.

4 Stitch along both clipped sides of the exterior, being sure to backstitch at the beginning and end.

5 Turn the bag exterior right side out and push the corners out using a chopstick or similar blunt object. Set the assembled exterior aside for now.

ASSEMBLING AND ATTACHING THE SLIP POCKET

1 Fold and press the 10" top edge of the slip pocket rectangle ½" to the wrong side. Press and repeat to enclose the top raw edge. Edgestitch along the fold.

2 Fold and press both 7" side edges a ½" to the wrong side. Repeat for the 10" bottom edge of the slip pocket so that all of the edges are now folded.

3 Center the assembled slip pocket from Step 2 on a lining panel 4½" away from the bottom edge and with both right sides facing up. Pin in place and topstitch around both sides and the bottom folds of the slip pocket. For a decorative touch, repeat with a second line of stitching ¼" away from the first.

4 Using a fabric marking pen and a ruler, draw a vertical line 2½" away from the pocket's right edge, along the full height of the attached slip pocket. This will be a divider for your pocket, so feel free to shift this line to a location that is appropriate for your purposes. Stitch along the drawn line backstitching at the beginning and end of the line of stitching. **(F)**

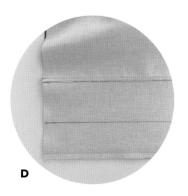

D

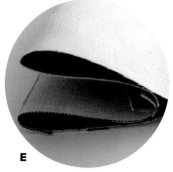

E

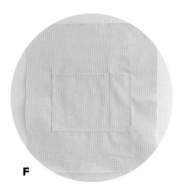

F

ASSEMBLING THE LINING

1 With the lining panels right sides together, pin or clip along the bottom edge only, leaving a 5" opening in the middle of the bottom seam for turning the bag through later. Be sure to backstitch at the beginning and end of the stitching line on both sides of the opening. Press the seams open.

2 Using a fabric marking pen and a ruler, mark a horizontal line on the wrong side of a lining panel, 2½" away from the bottom sewn edge from Step 1. Repeat on the other side of the lining panel on the wrong side.

3 Fold in both lining panels right sides together along the 2½" drawn lines from Step 2, just as you did for the exterior assembly. The bottom seam will now be between the right sides of the lining panels. Pin or clip along both long sides to prevent shifting.

4 Stitch along both clipped sides of the ;ining, being sure to backstitch at the beginning and end. **(I)**

FINISHING

1 With the right sides together and the lining still the wrong side out, insert the assembled exterior into the assembled lining with the opening in the bottom seam. **(J)**

2 Align the top raw edges of the exterior and the lining, making sure the casing and handles are lying nice and flat against the right side of the exterior panels and tucked inside.

3 Align the side seams of the exterior and the lining, nesting them together. Pin or clip around the circumference of the bag along the top raw edges. **(K)**

4 Stitch around the pinned or clipped top of the bag using a ¼" seam allowance. Where the leather handles are being attached, go back and forth a few times inside the seam allowance to firmly secure the handles.

5 Turn the bag right side out through the opening in the lining. Stitch the hole in the lining closed and gently push the lining inside the tote.

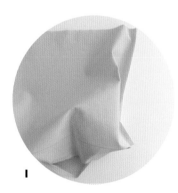
I

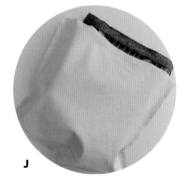
J

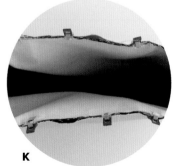
K

6 Push and press the exterior and the lining down and away from the casing. Pin through both layers to hold them in place being sure that the handles are extending up above the fold of the casing and not touching the exterior panels. Topstitch along the entire edge of the exterior fabric just below the seam between the casing and handles to secure all the layers together. **(L)**

7 Using a large safety pin at one end to help guide the ribbon, string the ribbon through the casing. Begin on the right side of the bag and bring the ribbon all the way around the top, passing through the left opening and coming out on the same side as you started. Securely knot the two ribbon ends together. **(M)**

8 String the second ribbon through the casing, this time starting and ending at the opposite side of the bag. Securely knot the two ribbon ends together as directed above.

9 Give your bag a final press along the sides and the folded bottom and you're finished. **(N)**

CUSTOMIZATION TIP

The casing options are endless. Try using leather strips, you can add a toggle at either end, use a thick cording or even make your own bias tape drawstring. Packing for a trip? Omit the leather handles entirely and you have a handy shoe bag that would fit at least two pairs!

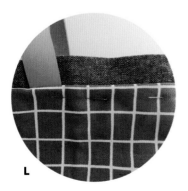

L

M

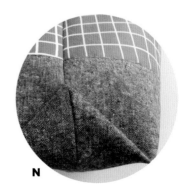

N

SOFT STORAGE BUCKET

These stylish storage buckets are perfect to keep random items throughout the house organized and easy to find when needed. Best of all, you can either use this as a bag, or fold the top edge a few inches over so that it functions as a full storage bucket.

FINISHED SIZE: 12" x 14"

SEAM ALLOWANCE: ½" unless otherwise noted

MATERIALS

½ yard of canvas (linen/cotton blend, or home décor fabric) for main exterior

1 yard of duck canvas for lining

1 yard of medium weight fusible interfacing

(2) 16" lengths of ¾" wide leather straps for the handles

(8) 6–8mm rivets

leather hole punch

rivet setting tool + mallet

fabric marking pen

pinking shears

CUTTING

Note: *measurements are width x height*

From the main exterior fabric, cut:
(1) 36" x 15" rectangle

From the lining fabric, cut:
(1) 36" x 15" rectangle
(2) 13" squares for exterior and lining base

From the interfacing, cut:
(1) 36" x 15" rectangle
(1) 13" square

ASSEMBLING THE EXTERIOR

1 With the right sides together, fold an exterior base lining square in quarters. Using the pattern on page 126, trace around the curve aligning the point of the wedge with the folded center of the lining. Cut along the drawn line. Repeat with the second lining square and the interfacing square

2 With one exterior base still folded in quarters, press to crease. Open the circle right side up and use a fabric marking pen to mark the four creases on the outside edge of the circle. These little marks will help with alignment of the bucket later. **(A)**

3 Following the manufacturer's instructions, fuse the interfacing to the wrong side of the main fabric panel and the exterior base lining circle.

4 With the right sides together, align the short edges of the main exterior panel, stitch and press the seam open **(B)**. With the panel still folded in half, mark the bottom side of the panel at the fold. Re-fold the panel, this time aligning the mark and the seam. Mark these two folds on the bottom edge of the main exterior panel to help with alignment.

5 With the right sides together, align the four marks on the exterior base with three marks and the side seam of the main exterior panel. Clip to hold in place at each mark. Add additional clips to securely attach the base to the main panel. Make sure to ease in both layers of the fabric evenly to avoid puckers. **(C)**

6 Sew the base to the main panel. Using pinking shears, trim the seam allowance to ¼". **(D)**

7 Turn the assembled exterior right side out, use your finger to push the seams from the inside to make the main seam as crisp as possible. Set the exterior aside for now.

8 Repeat Steps 4-7 to assemble the lining.

FINISHING

1 With the lining still wrong side out, insert the assembled exterior into the lining with the right sides together. Align the top raw edges as well as the seams of the exterior panel and the lining. Clip around the top edge of the bucket. **(E)**

2 Stitch around the top of the bucket leaving an 8" unsewn opening along the top of the bucket for turning.

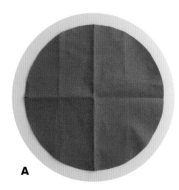

A

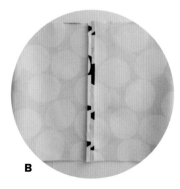

B

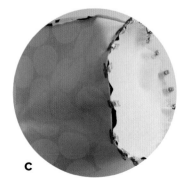

C

3 Press the top seam open and turn the bucket right side out through the opening in the top seam. Gently push the lining inside the bucket's exterior. Line up both panels and roll the top seam between your fingers to make it nice and crisp. Clip or pin around the top of the bucket, closing the opening as well.

4 Edgestitch all the way around the fold of the top seam.

5 Mark the placement of two vertical rivet holes on both sides of each leather strap, centering one a ¼" from the short end and a second ¾" from short end. Use a leather hole punch to cut the holes. Repeat for the second handle.

6 Fold the top edge of the bucket in half and pinch it gently to create a crease on the front and back sides of the bucket opening. Mark near the top edge, 2½" away from the crease on both sides.

7 Position one handle wrong side up 1½" from the top seam. Align the inner edges of the handle with the 2½" marks from Step 6. There will be a 5" gap between the inner edges of the handle. Make sure there are no twists. **(F)**

8 Keeping the handle at a 90 degree angle, use the four holes in your handle from Step 5 to mark the rivet placements. Move aside the handle and use a leather hole punch to make holes through both the exterior and the lining.

9 Attach the handle using rivets and following the instructions on page 15. Repeat Steps 7-8 to attach the second handle to the other side of the bucket.

CUSTOMIZATION TIP

Adding labels to these buckets is easy! Stamp out your word on a piece of twill tape. Fold over each of the short raw ends and center it over a leather rectangle roughly 1½ times the size. Use a leather needle and thick cotton thread to attach the tape to the leather and then the leather to the finished bag.

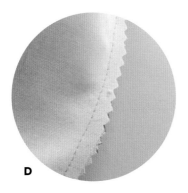

D

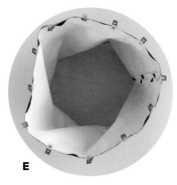

E

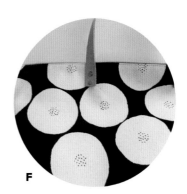

F

FOR
YOUR
PET

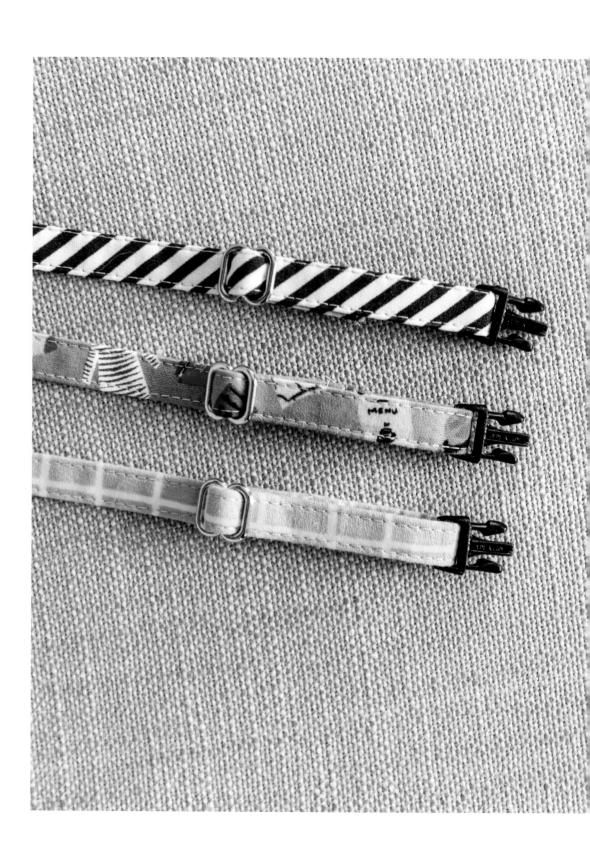

PREPPY COLLAR

These adjustable kitty collars are not only super cute, they are also lightweight and comfortable for your furry baby to wear. Just make sure to get the breakaway collar hardware to ensure your cat will always be safe when roaming around.

FINISHED SIZE: $3/8$" wide x up to 10" long

MATERIALS

(1) $1\frac{3}{4}$" x 15" strip of quilting cotton

(1) $7/8$" x 14" strip of medium weight fusible interfacing

(1) $3/8$" breakaway collar hardware - side release buckle, D-ring and bell, tri-slider

fabric marking pen

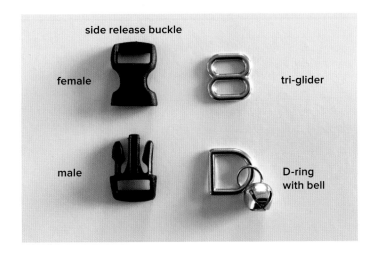

ASSEMBLING THE COLLAR STRAP

1 With the wrong sides together, fold the quilting cotton strip in half lengthwise and press. Open the strip and center the interfacing on the wrong side of one half of the collar strip. There will be ½" of fabric on each short end uncovered by the interfacing. Following the manufacturer's instructions, fuse in place.

2 With the wrong sides together, fold and press a short edge of the fused strip ½" to the wrong side. Repeat for the second short edge. Press the long raw edges towards the center crease from Step 1.

3 Refold the strip in half again, enclosing the raw edges. Press the strip once and pin or clip in place. **(A)**

4 Edgestitch around all four sides of the fused collar encasing all of the raw edges.

ATTACHING THE HARDWARE

1 Place the edgestitched collar right side up on your work surface. Use a fabric marking pen and a ruler to make a mark 1½" from both short ends.

2 Thread one short end of the collar over the middle bar of the tri-slider so the bar is directly over the 1½" mark on the strap. Fold the strap back over the bar and edgestitch in place. Then stitch along the short edge over the existing line of edgestitching, backstitching at the beginning and end. Repeat another line of edgestitching ¼" away from the first.

3 Thread the opposite short end of the strap through the male part of the buckle. The prongs will be on the top side of the strap facing away from the tri-slider. **(B)**

4 Continue to thread the strap through the tri-slider, over the middle bar and double-stitched strap end. **(C)**

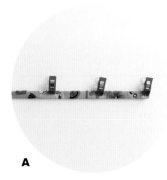

A

B

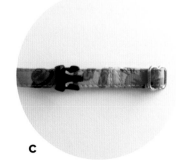

C

5 Continue threading the short end through the D-ring and the female part of the buckle, so the female opening is facing opposite the prongs of the male buckle on the other end of the collar. **(D)**

6 Align the middle bar of the buckle with the other 1½" mark. Fold the strap at the 1½" mark to the wrong side. Stitch the short end in place. The buckle and the D-ring should both be secured within the loop. **(E)**

7 Slide the D-ring close to the stitches from the previous step, and make one more line of stitches between the buckle and D-ring approximately ½" away from the previous line of stitching. **(F)**

8 Adjust the collar to fit comfortably around your pet's neck and you're all finished.

CUSTOMIZATION TIP
You could definitely make this collar for your dog as well. Simply adjust the size of the collar strap by cutting it 4 times the width of the hardware x the length needed depending on the size of your dog's neck. ¾"–1" wide hardware should work great!

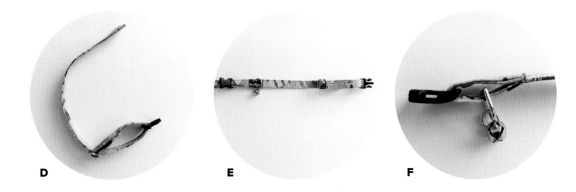

D　　　　**E**　　　　**F**

CATNIP FISH

These catnip-filled kicker toys are just the right size for your kitty to hug, chase, or snuggle with while playing. Just make sure to fill it firmly with the polyfilll and add a good amount of catnip to stimulate your cat's hunting instincts.

FINISHED SIZE: 10" x 3"

MATERIALS

Note: *Materials listed make one fish*

(1) 2½" x 4½" rectangle for the head

(1) 7" x 4½" rectangle for the main body

(1) 2½" x 4½" rectangle for the tail

(1) 11" x 4½" rectangle for the back

3 tablespoons of catnip

polyfilll

hand sewing supplies

black perle cotton, embroidery thread, or permanent marker for the eye

fabric marking pen

ASSEMBLING THE FISH

1 Stitch the head and tail rectangles to opposite ends of the main body rectangle along the 4½" edges. Press the seams towards the darker fabric. This is the front panel.

2 With the front and back panels right sides together, align all of the raw edges. Photocopy the pattern on page 127 to use as a template. Align the head and tail printed lines on the pattern with the seams on the front panel and use a fabric pen to outline the template. **(A)**

3 Remove the template carefully and add a few pins through both back and front panels inside the drawn line. These will hold the fabrics in place as you sew. **(B)**

4 Backstitching at both the beginning and end, stitch along the drawn line, leaving a 3" opening along the bottom seam. Use a pair of sharp fabric scissors to cut away the excess fabric, leaving a ¼" seam allowance. Make small snips into the seam allowance all the way around the outline taking care not to cut into the stitches. **(C)**

5 Turn the fish right side out through the opening and use a chopstick or similar blunt object to neatly push the tail fabric out.

6 Stuff the tail and head with polyfilll first, add the catnip and then finish stuffing with more polyfilll until the fish is nice and firm. **(D)**

7 Neatly fold the opening closed, use pins or sewing clips to hold the layers in place and hand stitch the opening closed. **(E)**

8 Use perle cotton, embroidery thread, or permanent marker to add the eye. **(F)**

CUSTOMIZATION TIP

Worried about your attack cat making a hole in the fish, creating a catnip disaster? Sew up a simple 3" muslin pouch. Sew around three sides, use a piece of paper to funnel in the catnip, then stitch the final edge and tuck it inside the fish.

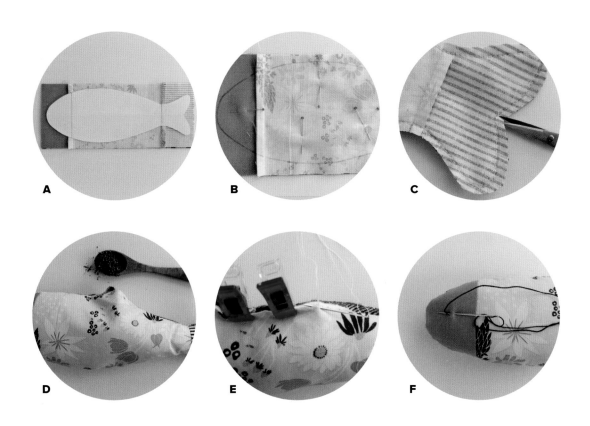

A   **B**   **C**

D   **E**   **F**

PET TEEPEE

When I couldn't find the right kind of cozy hiding spot for our two furry girls, I decided to make a pet teepee for them myself. I used neutral fabric to fit in with our home décor, but you could definitely go with bold, bright colors if that's what makes your heart sing. I recommend using a canvas or home décor weight fabric to give the teepee some body.

FINISHED SIZE: approx. 20" square bottom x 30" tall

MATERIALS

1½ yards of main fabric if using 54" wide fabric or 2¼ yards if using 42" wide fabric

½ yard of contrasting fabric for dowel casings

(4) 36" long, ½" diameter dowels

36" length of strong twine, string, or leather lace

fabric marking pen

washi tape (optional)

CUTTING

From the main fabric, cut:

(5) panels using the illustrations below. Draw a pattern directly onto the main fabric using a fabric marking pen and a ruler. Cut three full main triangle panels and one of each of the half triangle front panels

From the contrasting casing fabric, cut:

(4) 3" tall x 25" wide strips

Note: *This is not intended to be a child's toy*

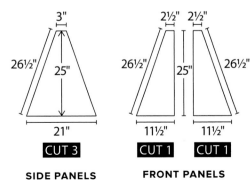

SIDE PANELS

FRONT PANELS

ASSEMBLING THE MAIN PANELS

1 Use either a zig zag stitch or overlock stitch to neatly finish the long edges of all of the front panels. **(A)**

2 Hem the top and bottom short edges on each of the five panels by folding and pressing the raw edge ¼" to the wrong side **(B)**. Fold over ¼" again and press. Topstitch along the double fold. **(C)**

3 On the wrong side of one front panel and beginning at the short folded edge, mark a perpendicular 6" line 1" away from the long edge and connect it back up to the long edge to form an 'L'. **(D)**

4 Pin the front panels right sides together and stitch them together along the 6" drawn line from Step 3 stopping at the perpendicular 1" mark. Be sure to backstitch at the beginning and end of the line of stitching. Press the seam open and continue to press a 1" fold along both lengths of the front panels.

5 Tuck the pressed seam allowance in half to encase the serged edge inside the folded hem and pin in place **(E)**. Edgestitch along the folded edge. Repeat for the opposite pressed edge.

6 Using a fabric marking pen, draw a ½" tall triangle and stitch around the drawn triangle to secure the opening. **(F)**

CREATING THE DOWEL CASINGS

1 Hem all the short edges of the casings, using the instructions in Step 2 above.

2 With the wrong sides together, fold one casing strip in half lengthwise and pin in place. Use a zigzag or overlock stitch to secure the edges. Repeat for the three remaining dowel casings. **(G)**

FINISHING

1 With the front panels right side up, center one dowel casing along the unhemmed edge and align the raw edges. There will be a ¾" portion of the front panel edge on either side which is not covered by the casing. **(H)**

2 Layer a main panel on top with the right sides facing. The dowel casing is nested in between the panels. **(I)**

3 Align the long edges and pin. Using a ½" seam allowance, stitch the layers together. There will be a bit of extra fabric along the bottom edge in the seam allowance. Just tuck the extra fabric under and stitch in place. Press. **(J)**

4 Repeat Steps 1-3 adding casings in between the main panels until all of the panels are stitched together.

5 Slide the dowels through the casings, one at a time. There should be about 2" of dowel sticking out on the bottom. Once all four dowels are in, place the teepee in a standing position and adjust the dowel placement. Use the strong twine or leather lace to secure the dowels together. The twine will be about 5-6" away from the top of the dowels. **(K)**

6 Apply a strip of washi tape to the dowels if desired. **(L)**

CUSTOMIZATION TIP

It may be tempting to use a novelty print for this fun tent. This is a large structure that makes a big statement, so be careful when selecting fabrics to choose colors that go well with your home.

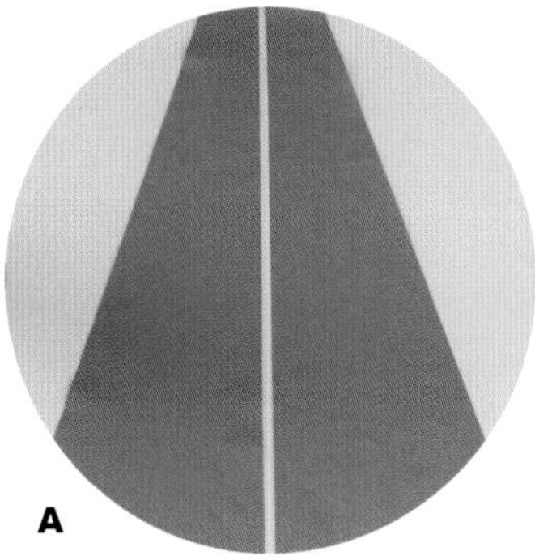

A

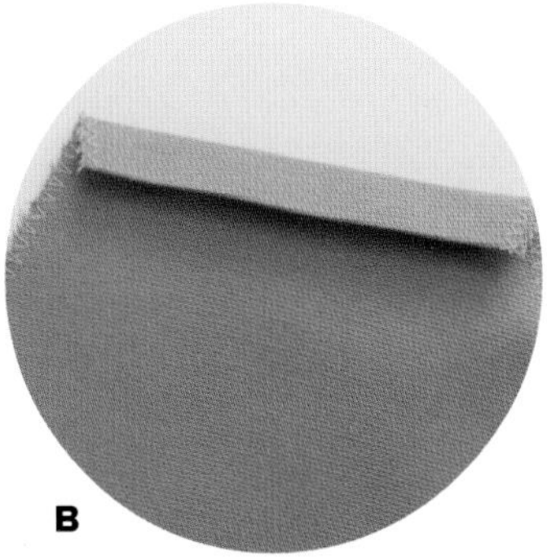

B

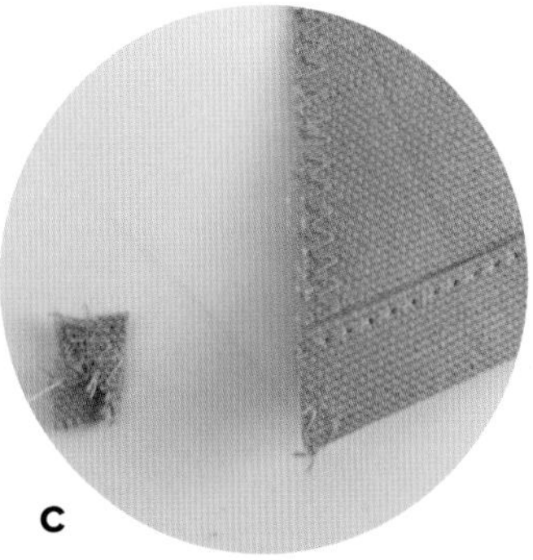

C

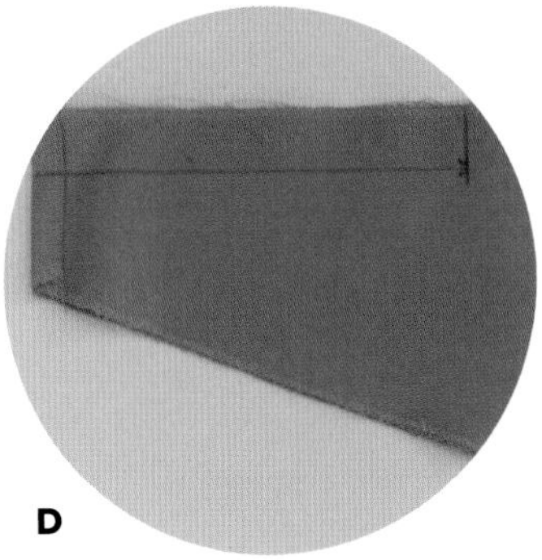

D

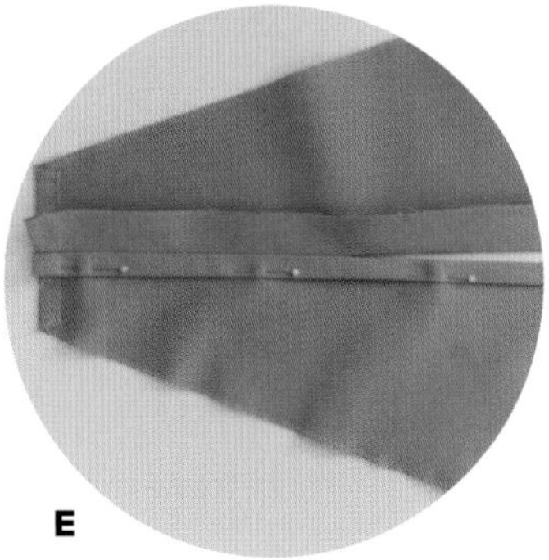

E

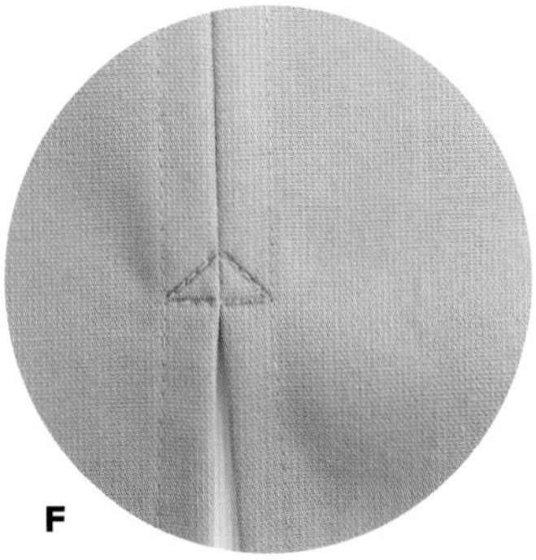

F

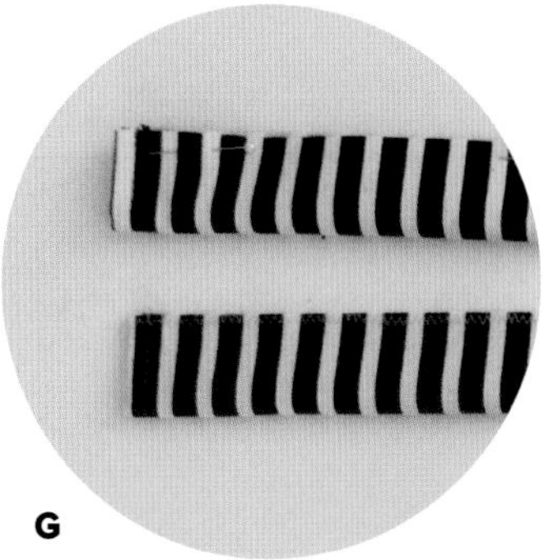

G

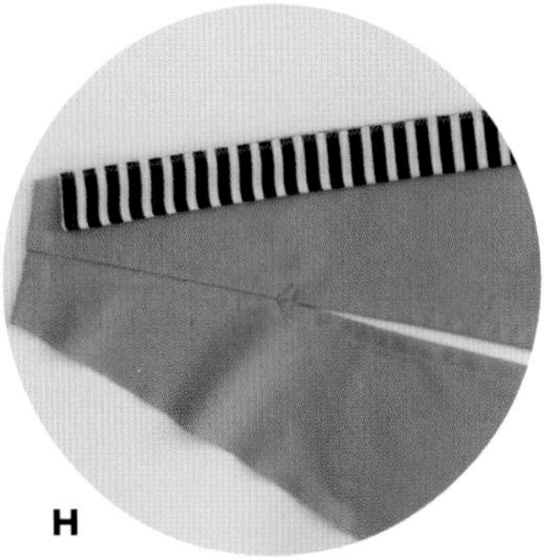

H

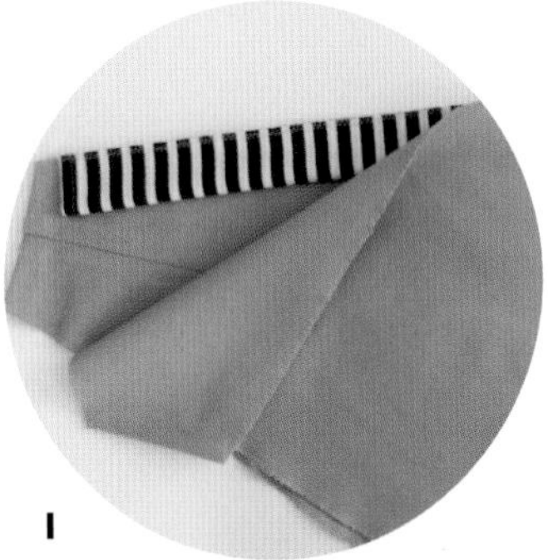

I

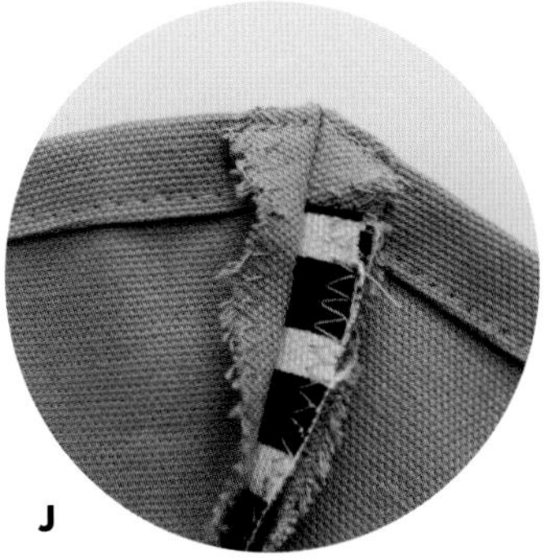

J

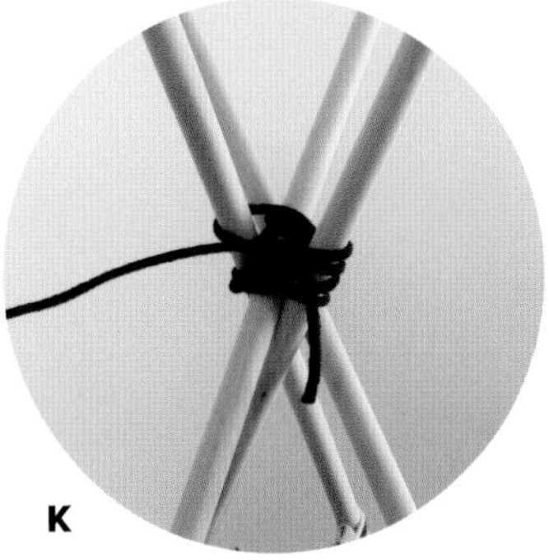

K

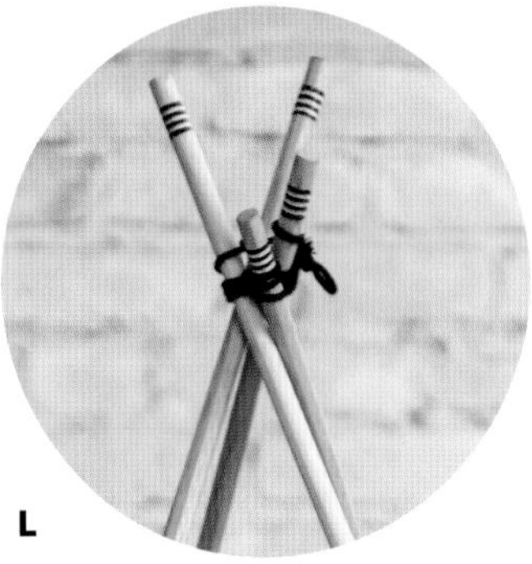

L

TEMPLATES

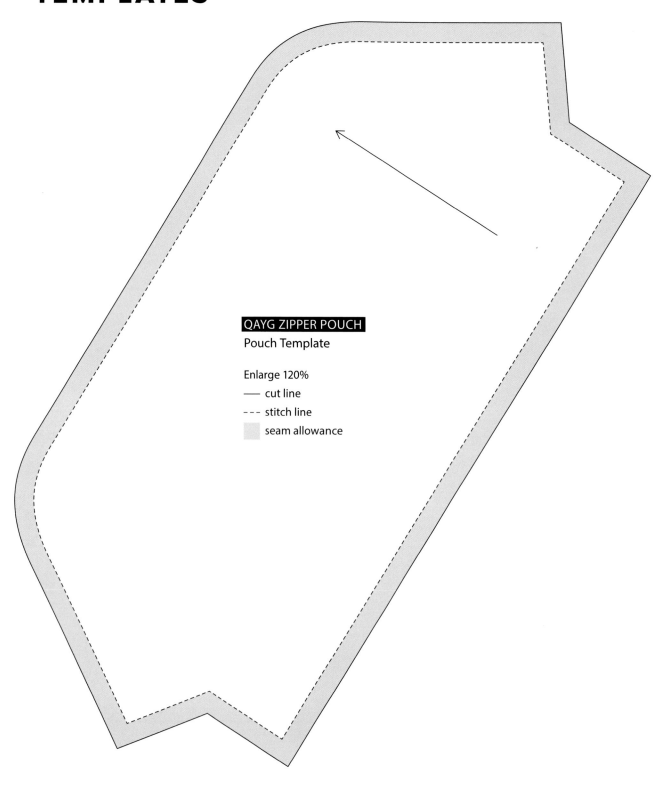

QAYG ZIPPER POUCH
Pouch Template

Enlarge 120%
—— cut line
- - - stitch line
seam allowance

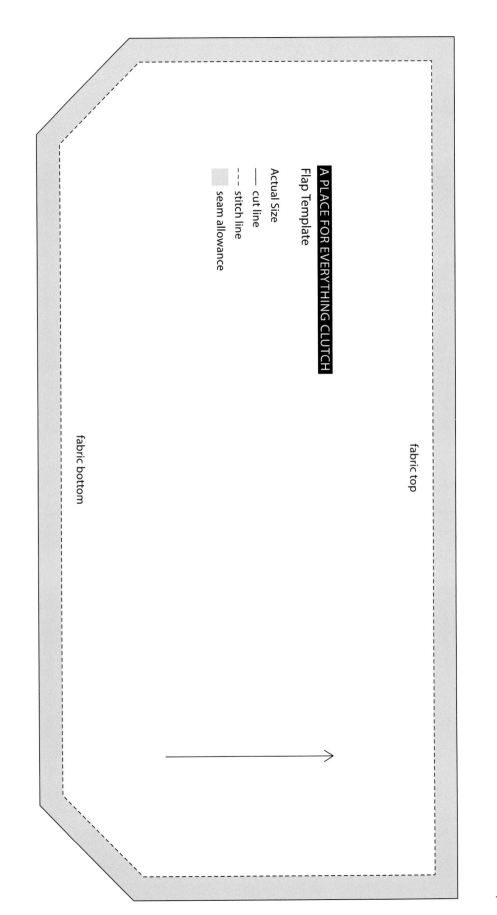

A PLACE FOR EVERYTHING CLUTCH

Flap Template

Actual Size

— cut line

--- stitch line

▨ seam allowance

fabric top

fabric bottom

BIG STITCH THROW PILLOWS
Quilting Template 1

Enlarge 200%

—— stitch line

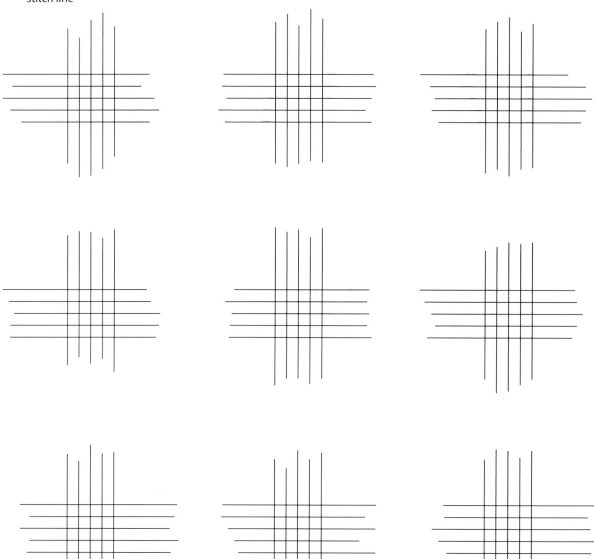

BIG STITCH THROW PILLOWS

Quilting Template 2

Enlarge 200%

—— stitch line

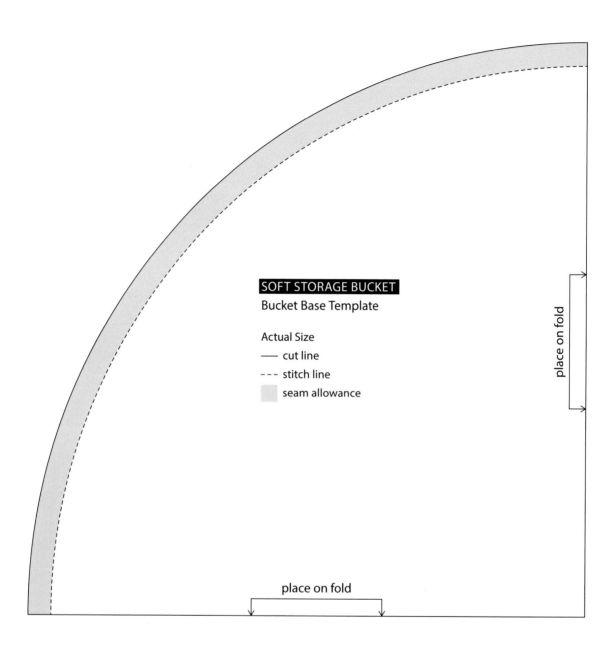

SOFT STORAGE BUCKET
Bucket Base Template

Actual Size
—— cut line
--- stitch line
▨ seam allowance

place on fold

place on fold

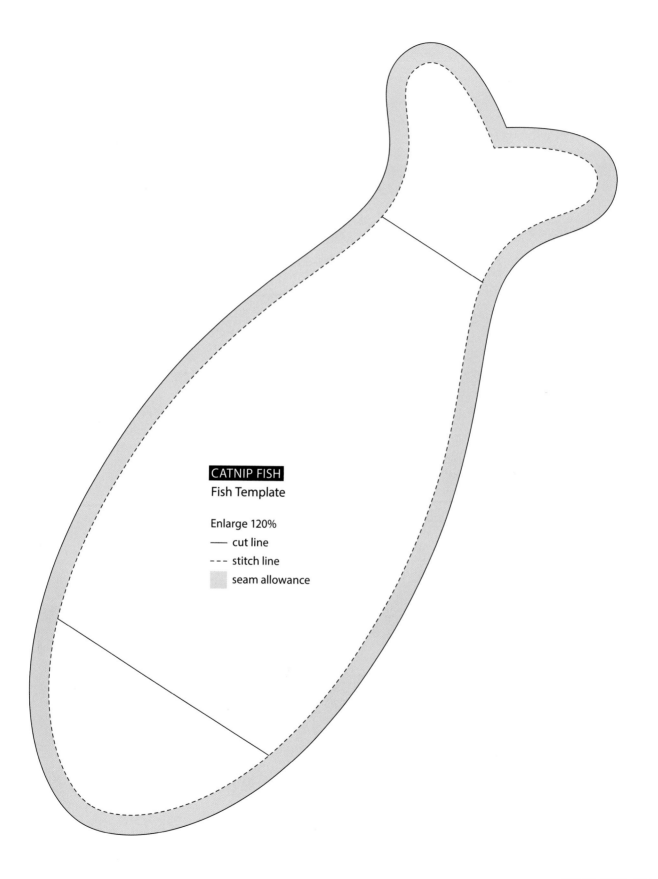

CATNIP FISH

Fish Template

Enlarge 120%

—— cut line

- - - stitch line

seam allowance